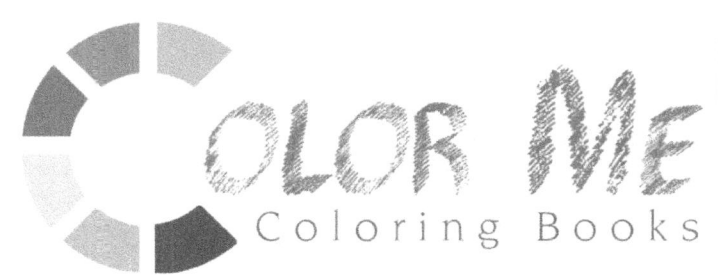

POLITICIANS

By

Kevin & Jody Dooley

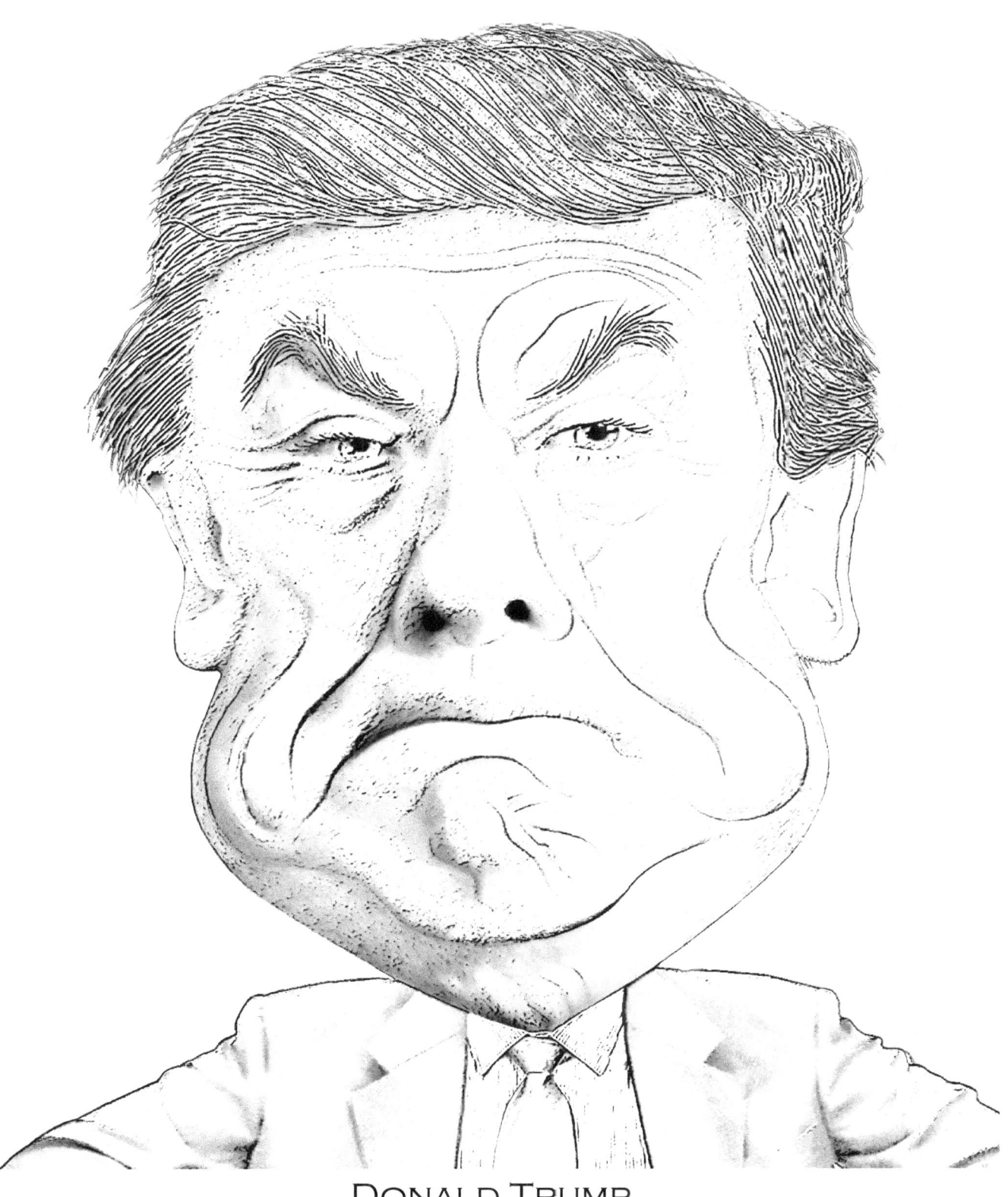

DONALD TRUMP

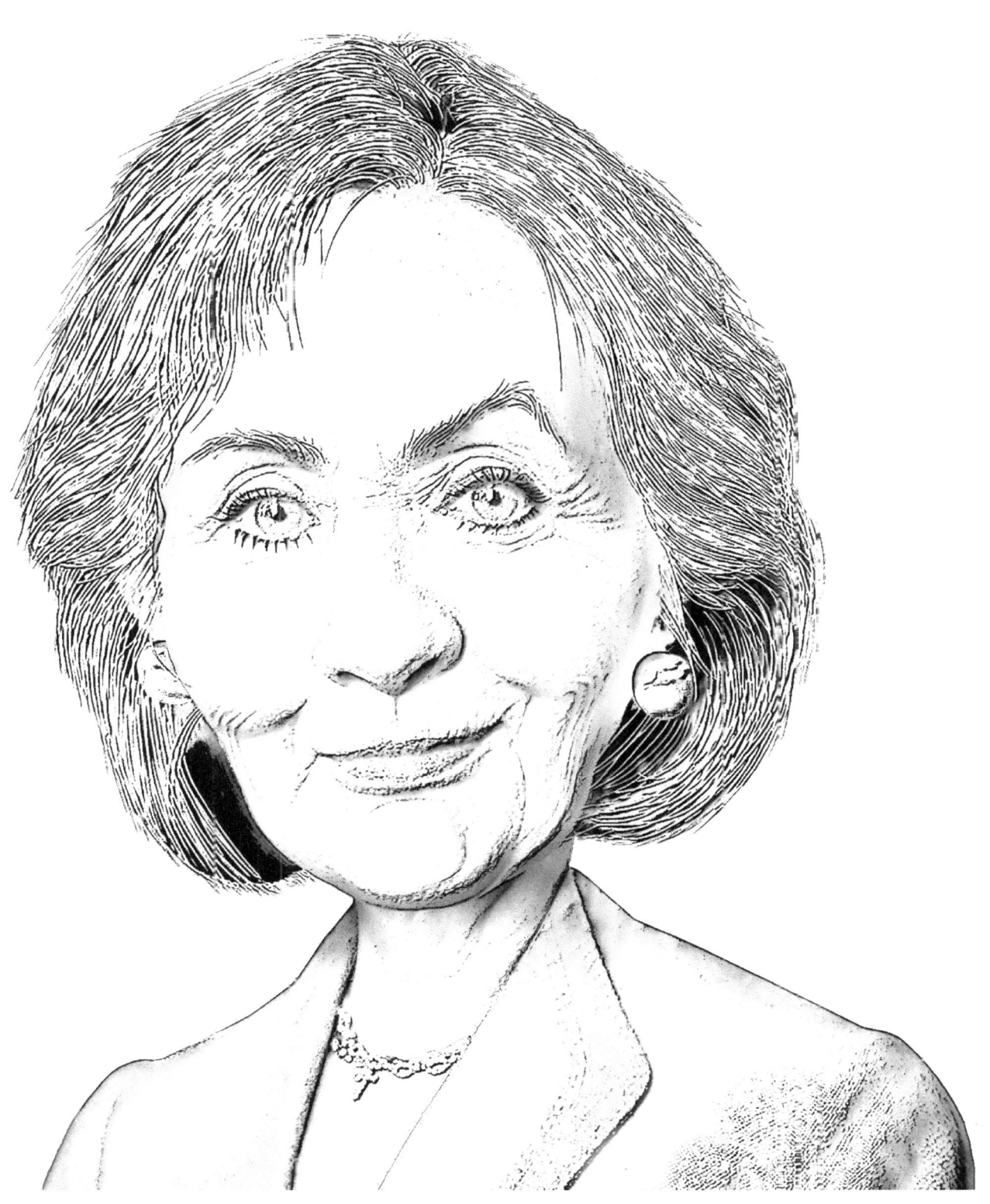

HILLARY CLINTON

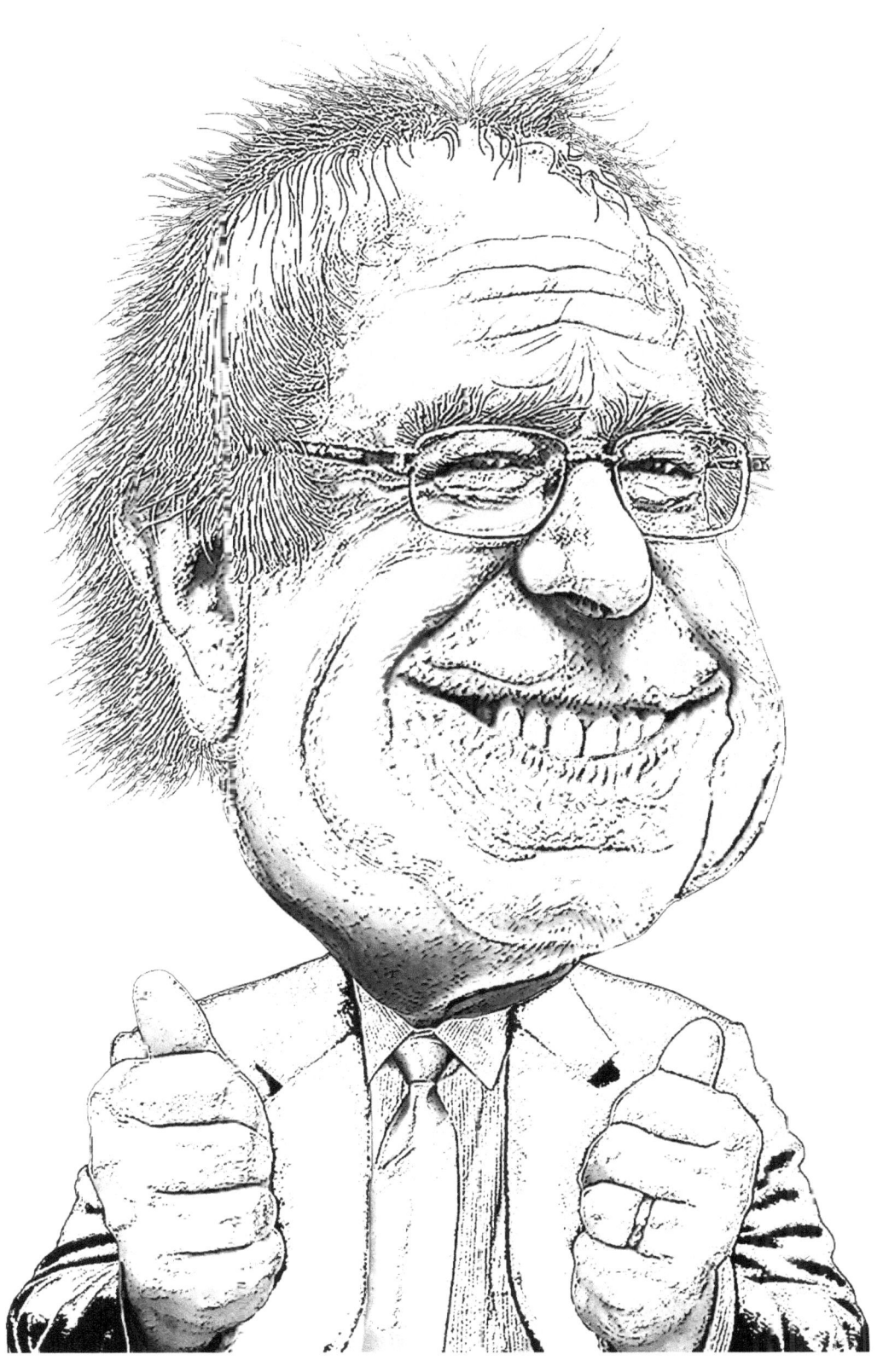

BERNIE SANDERS

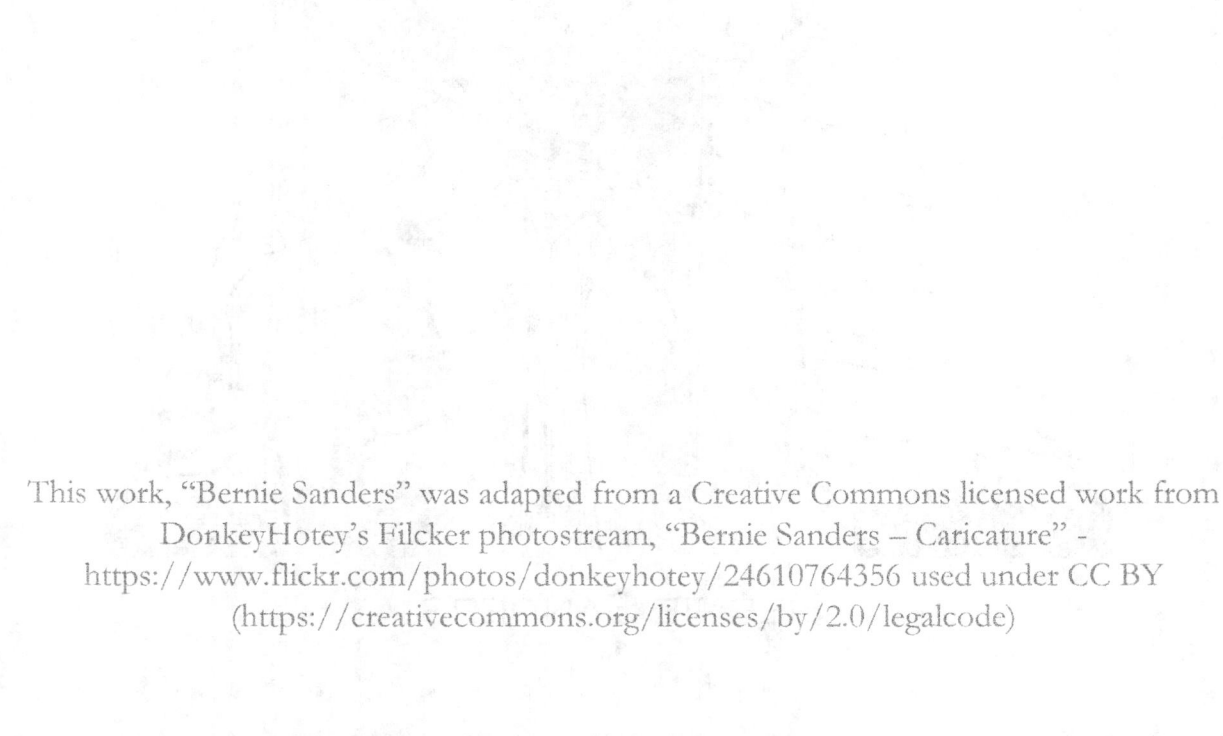

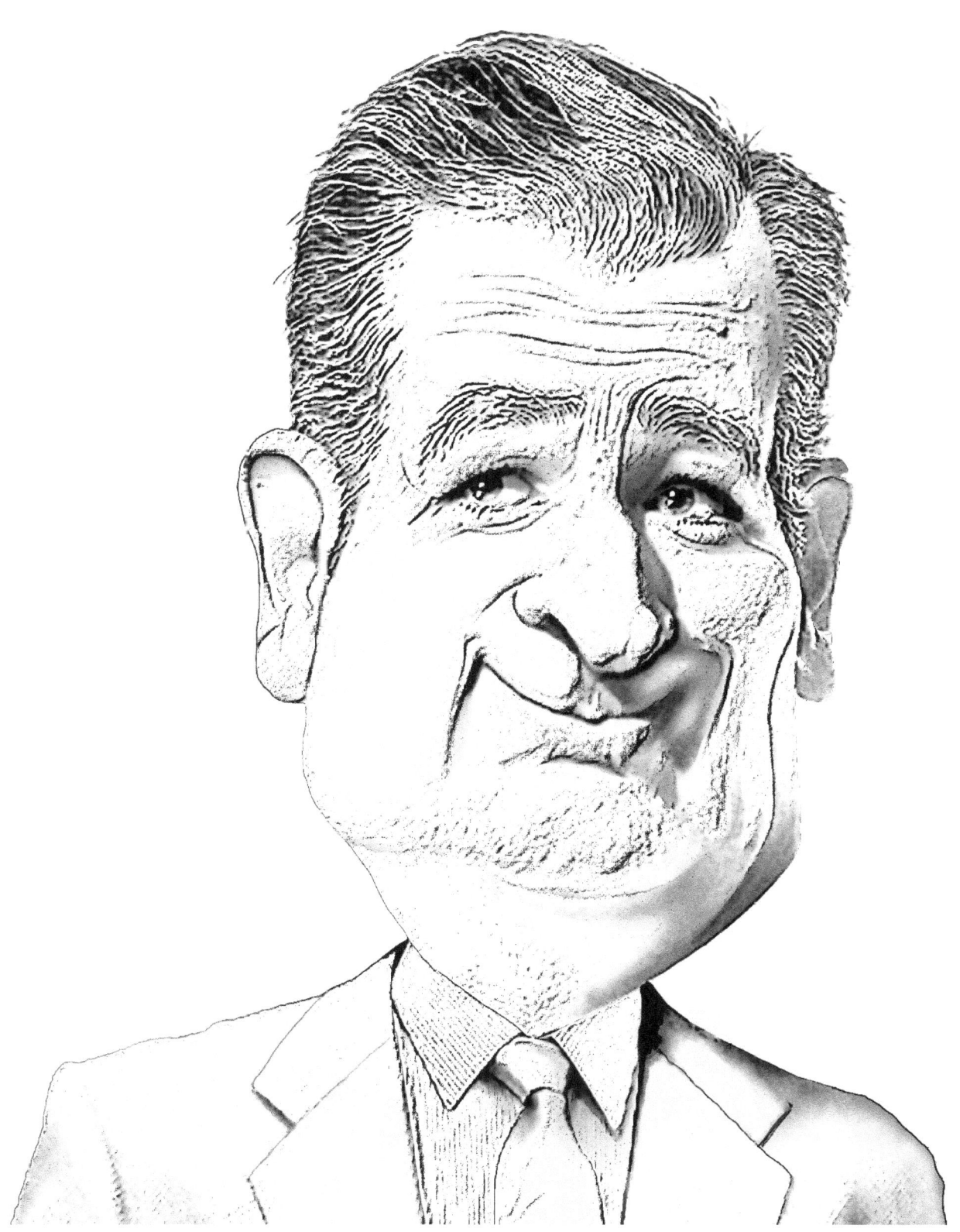

TED CRUZ

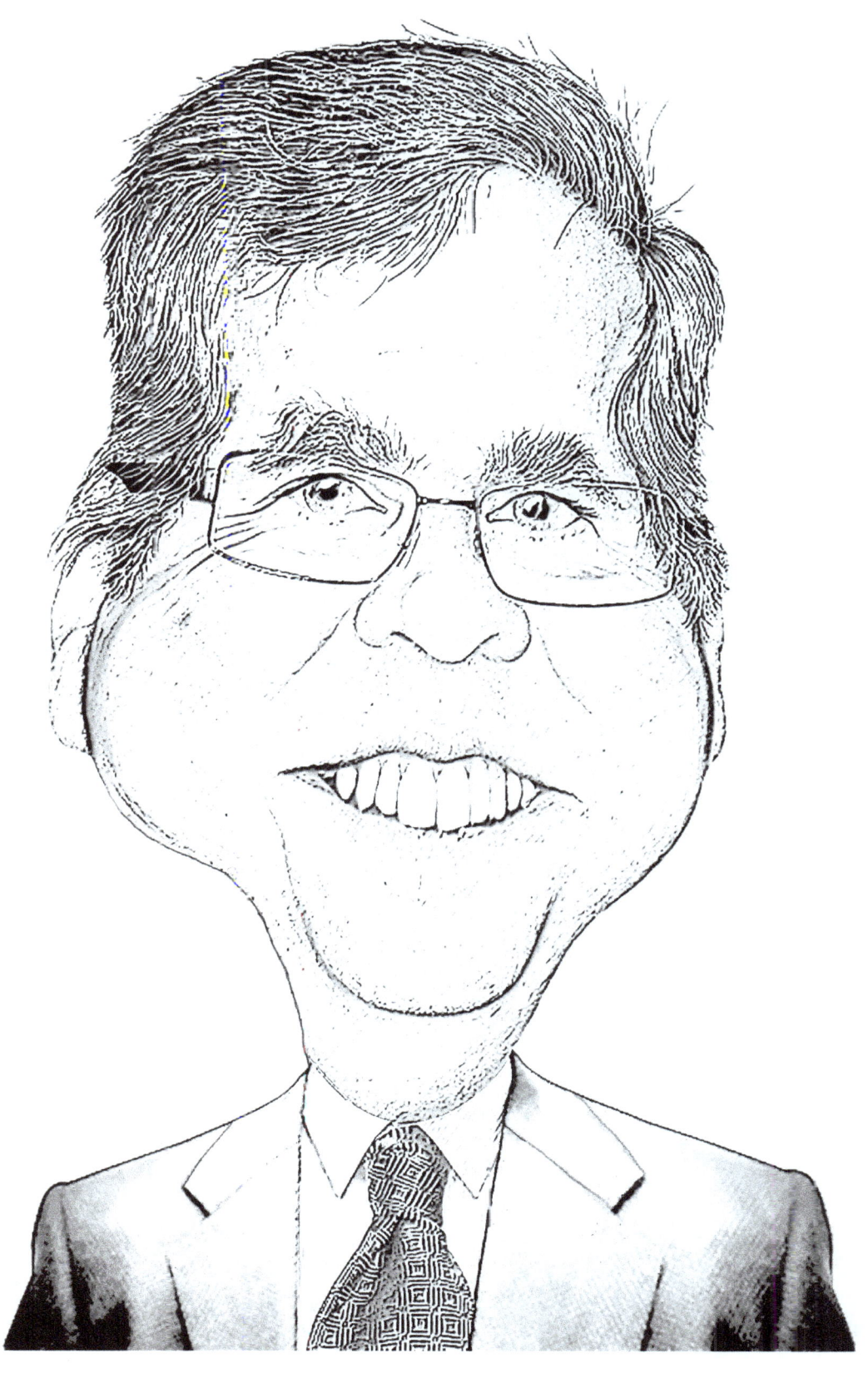

JEB BUSH

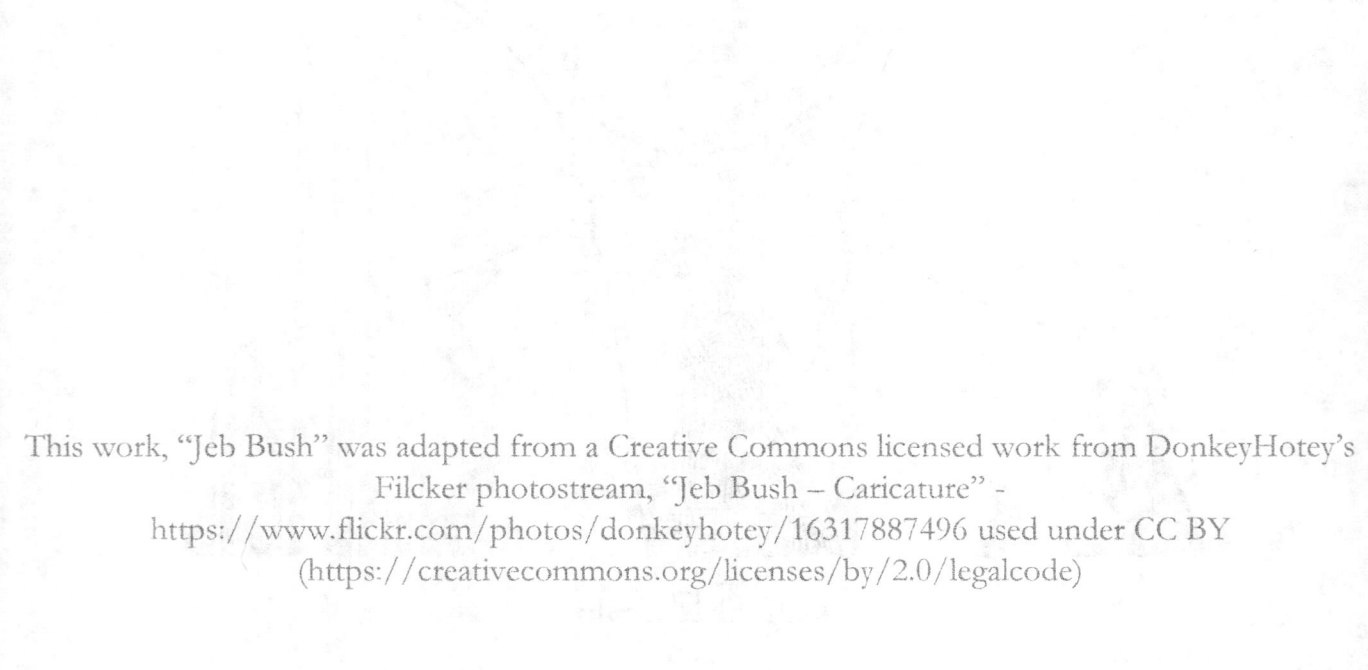

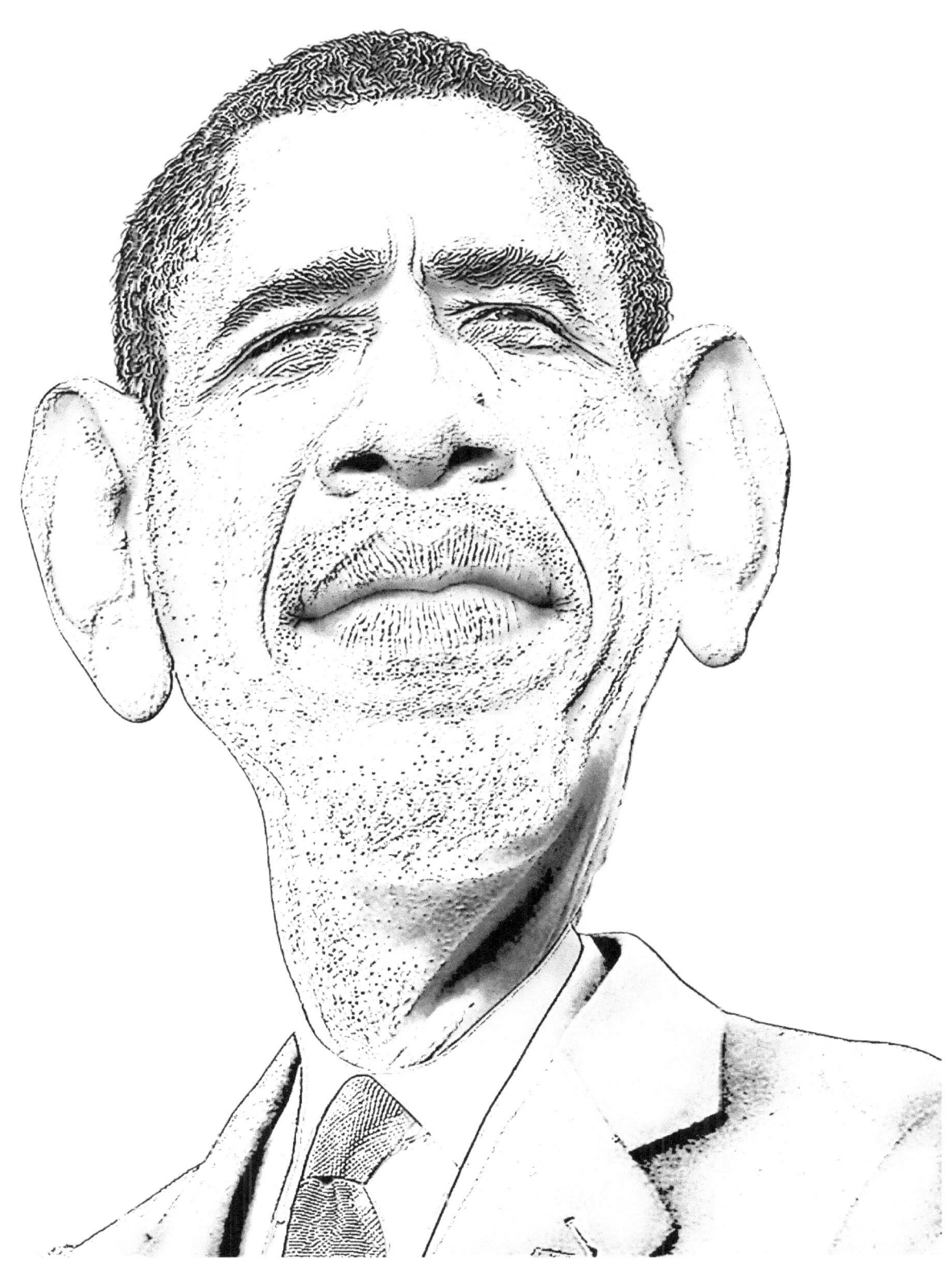

BARACK OBAMA

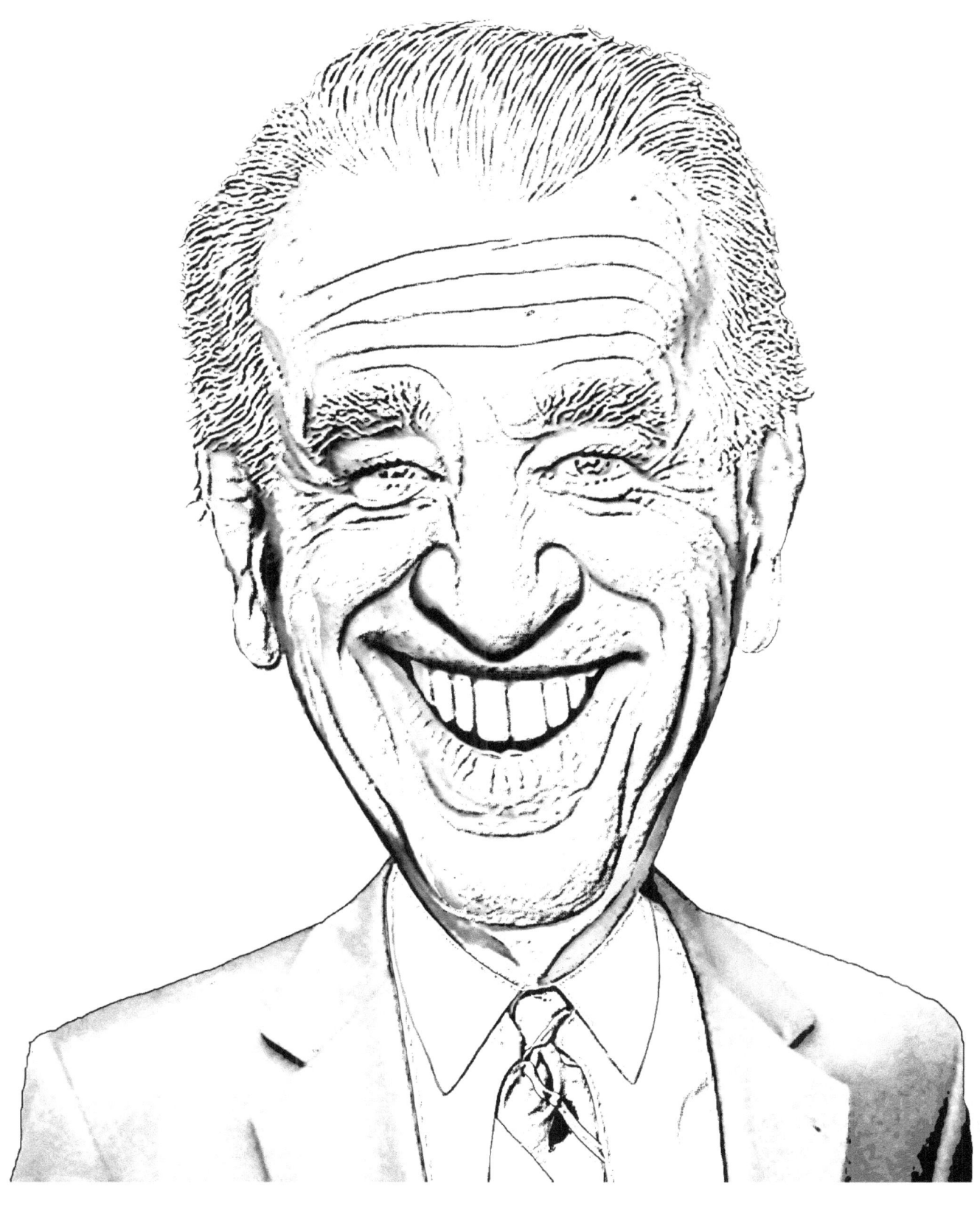

JOE BIDEN

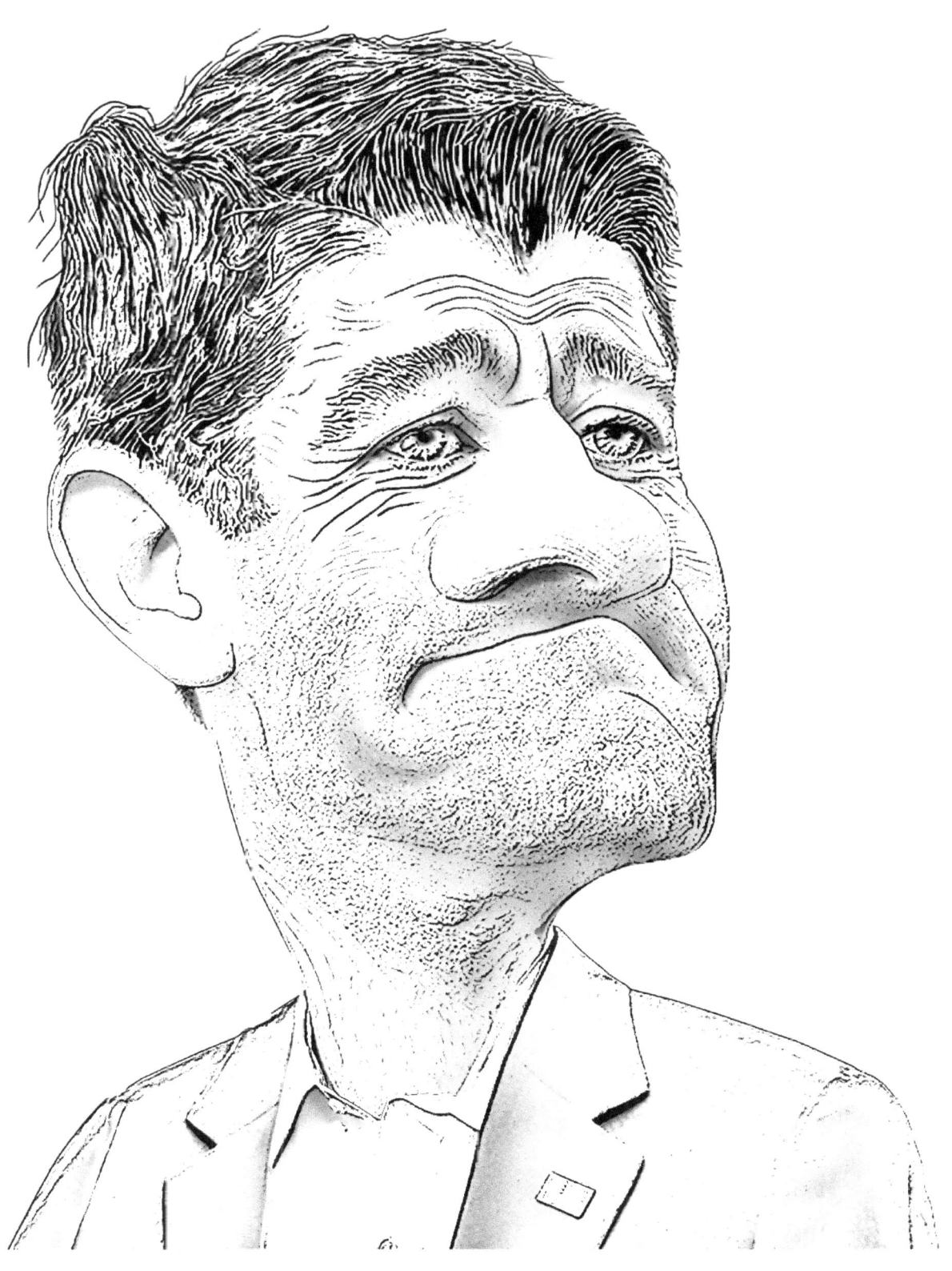

PAUL RYAN

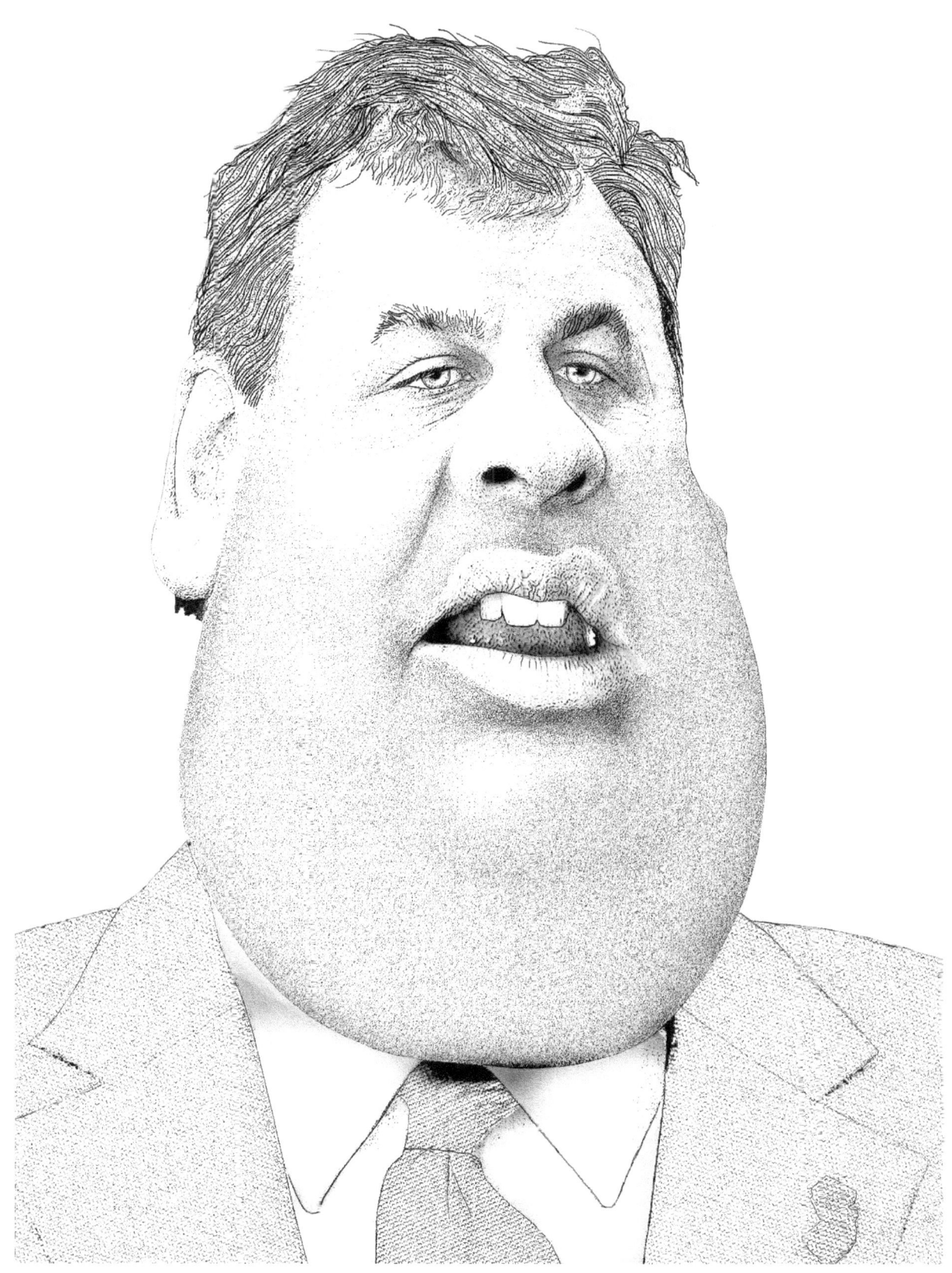

CHRIS CHRISTIE

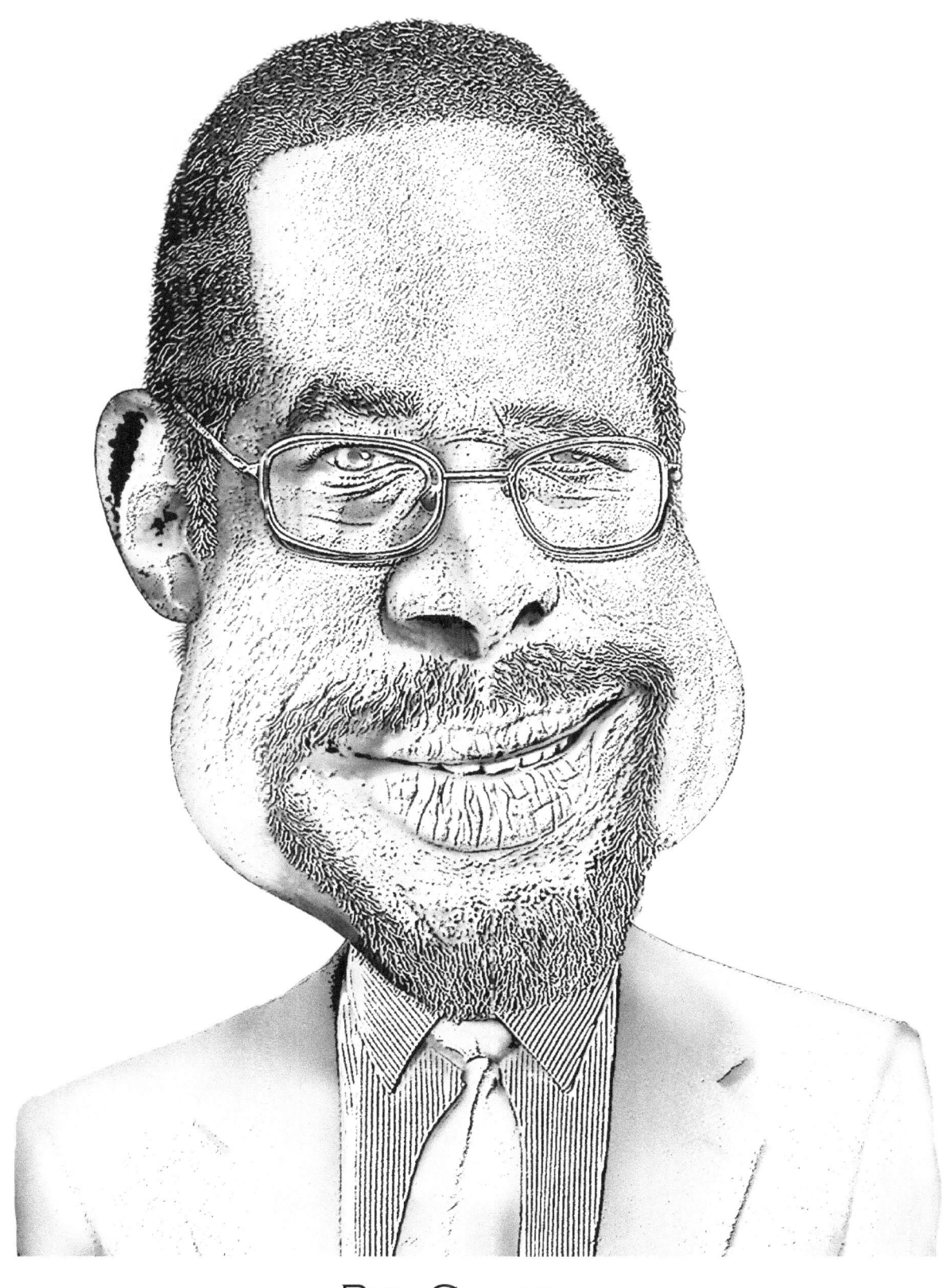

BEN CARSON

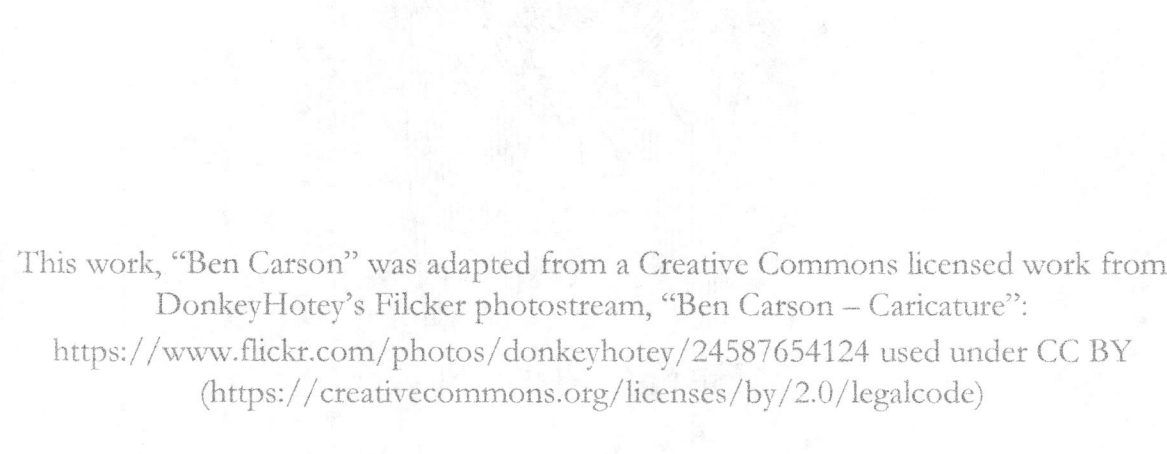

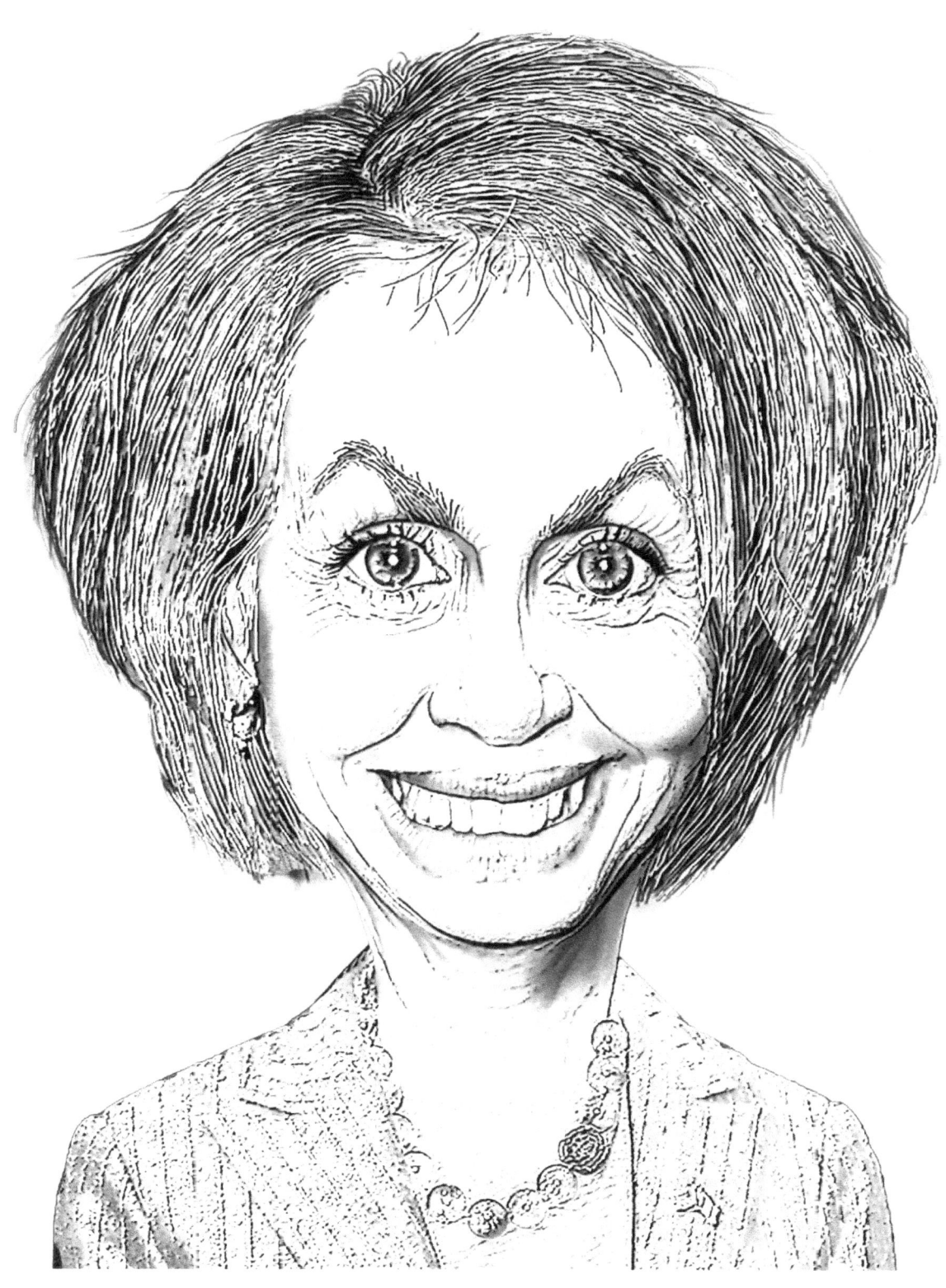

NANCY PELOSI

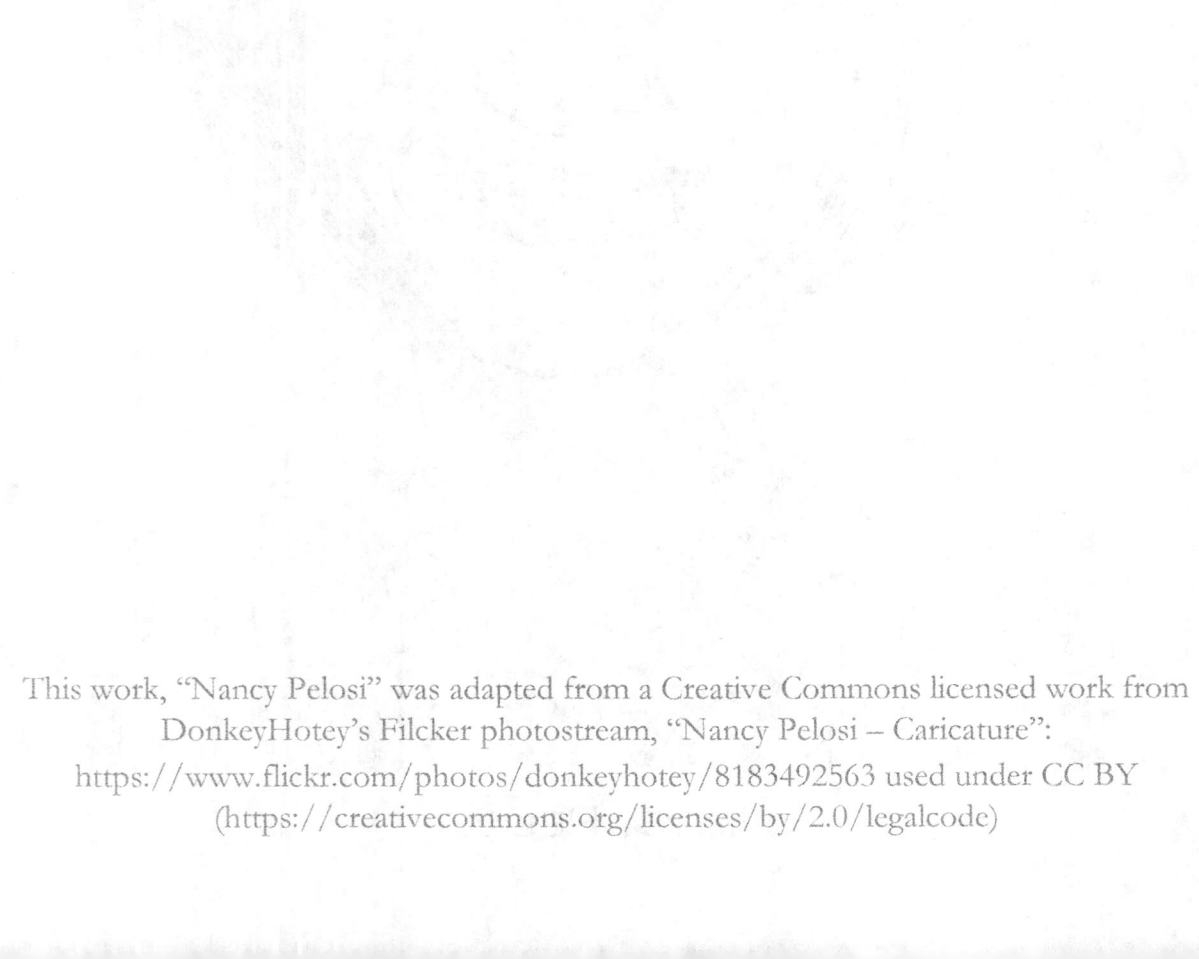

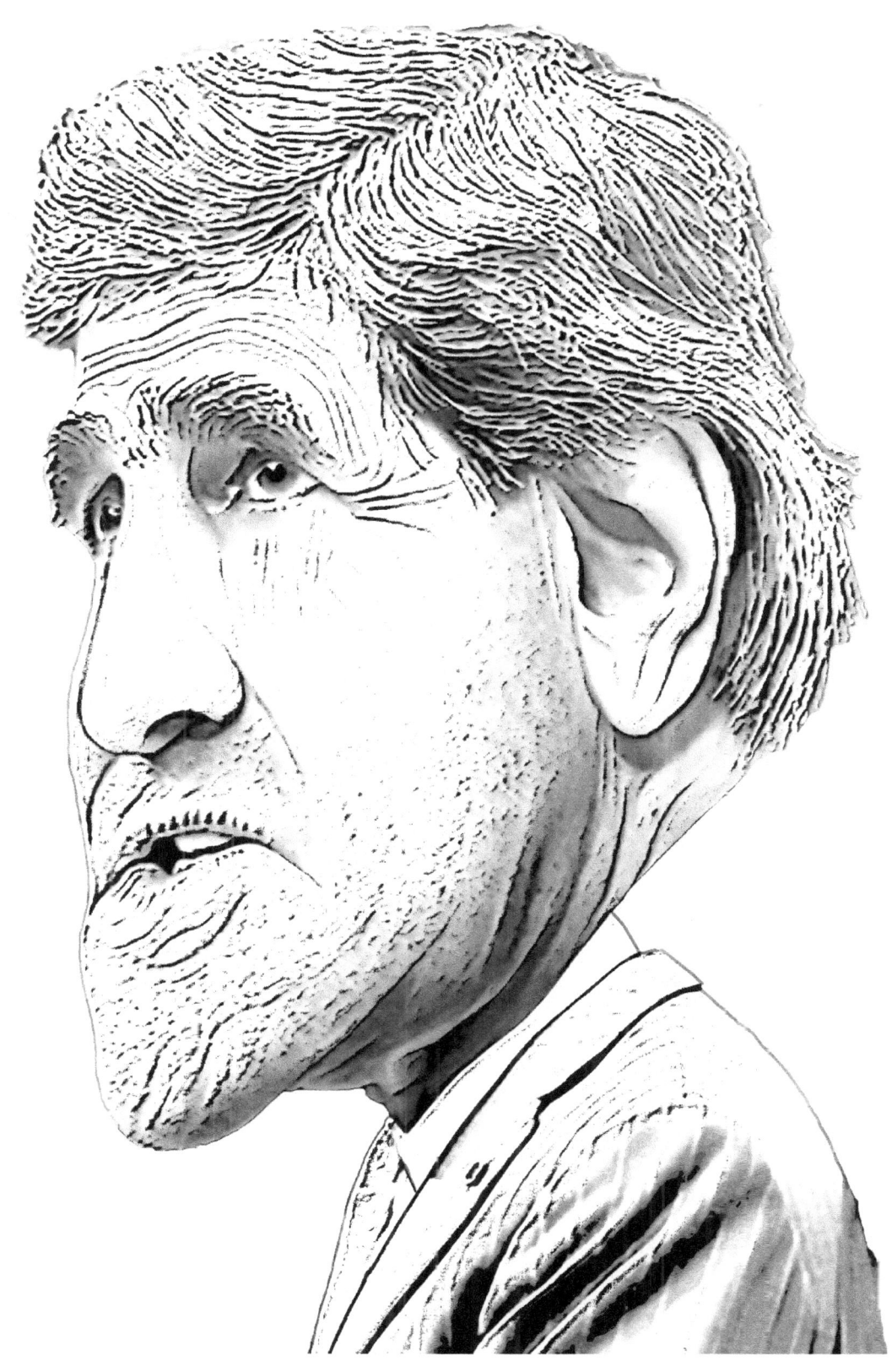

JOHN KERRY

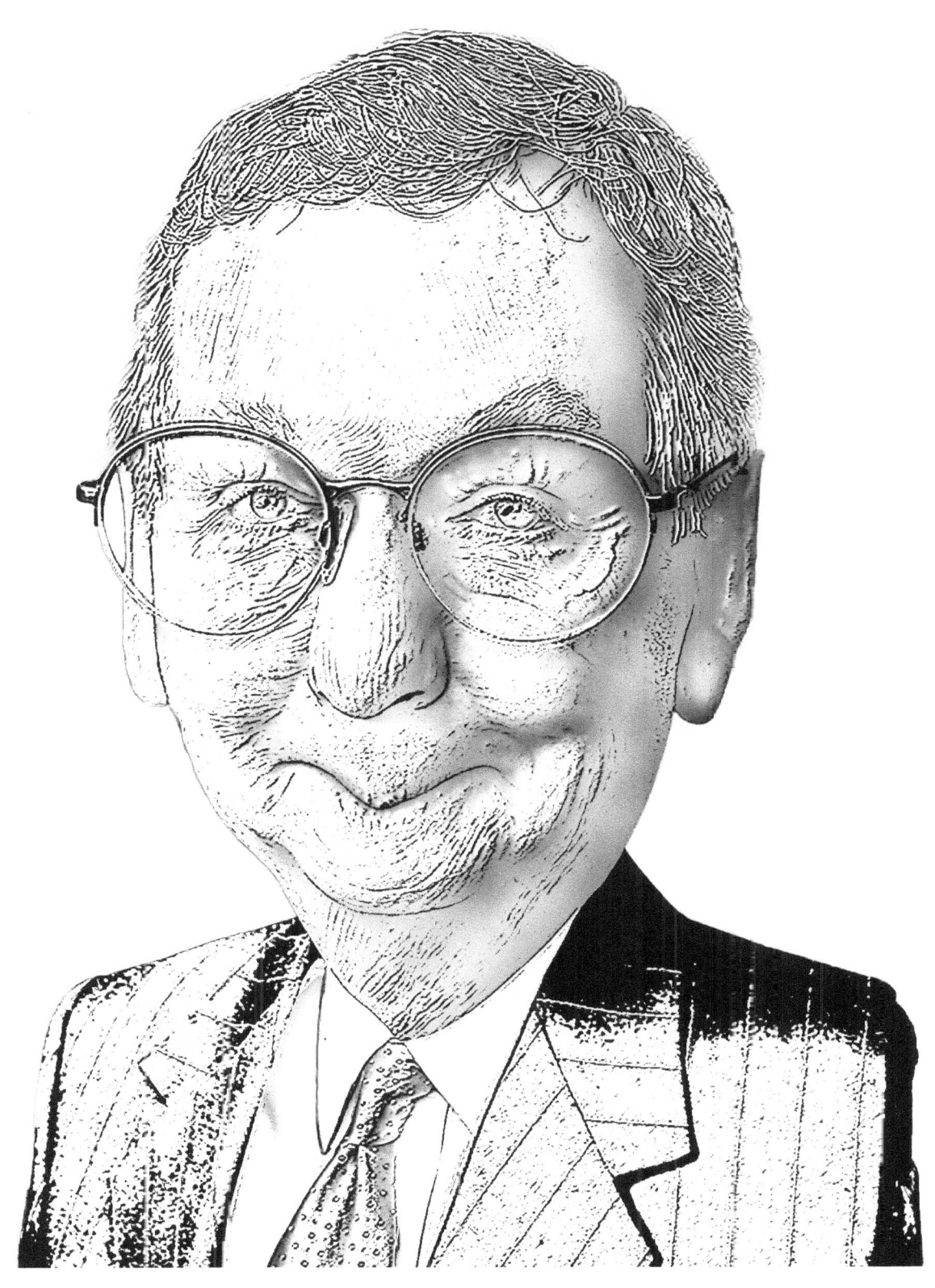

MITCH MCCONNELL

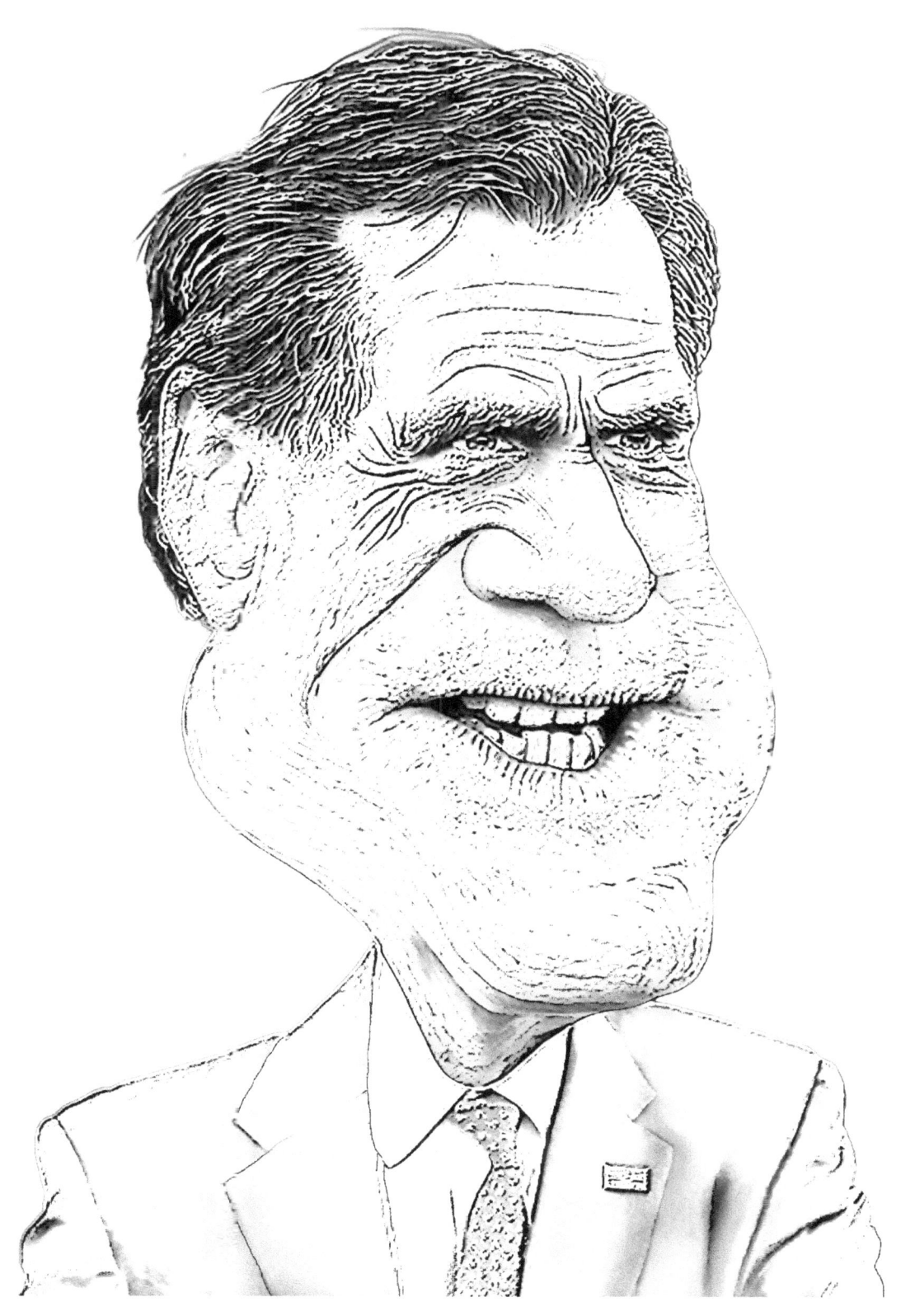

MITT ROMNEY

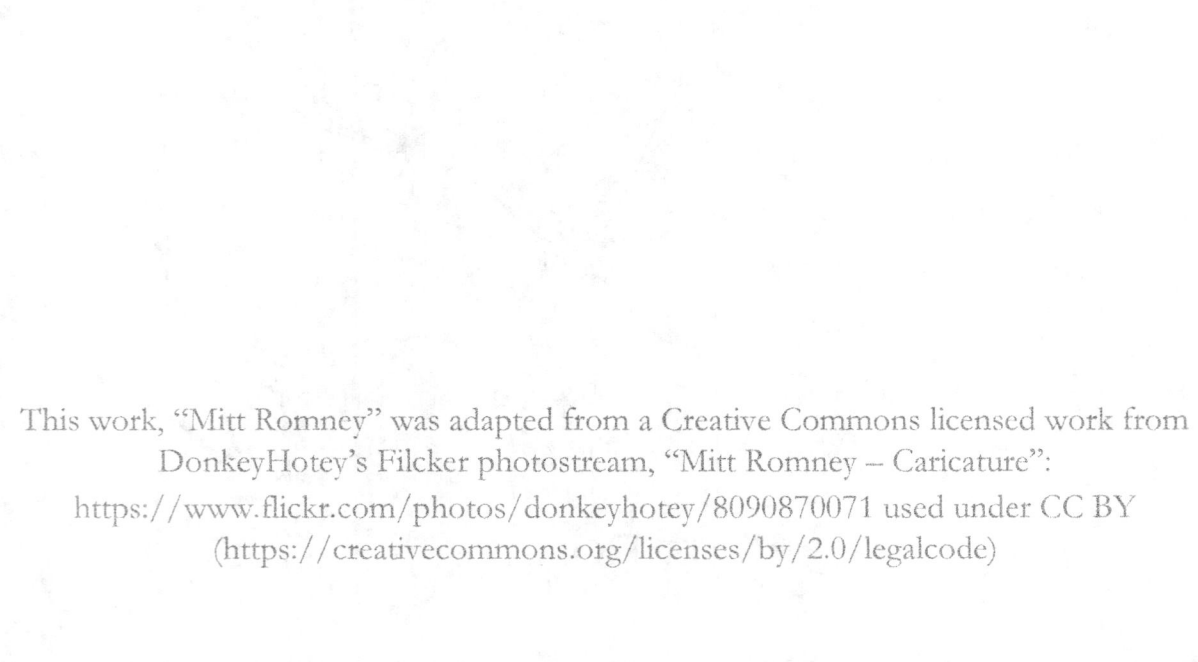

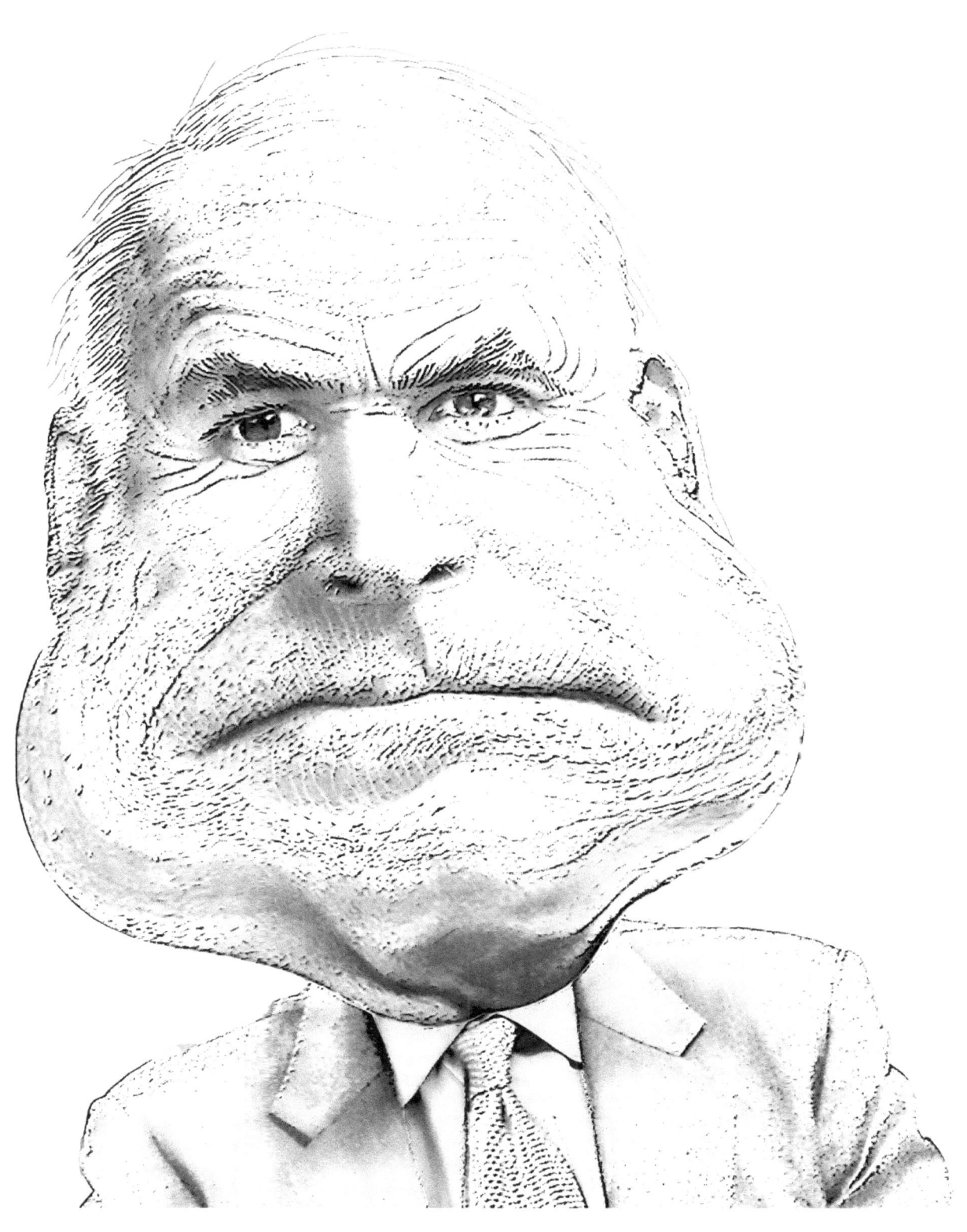

JOHN MCCAIN

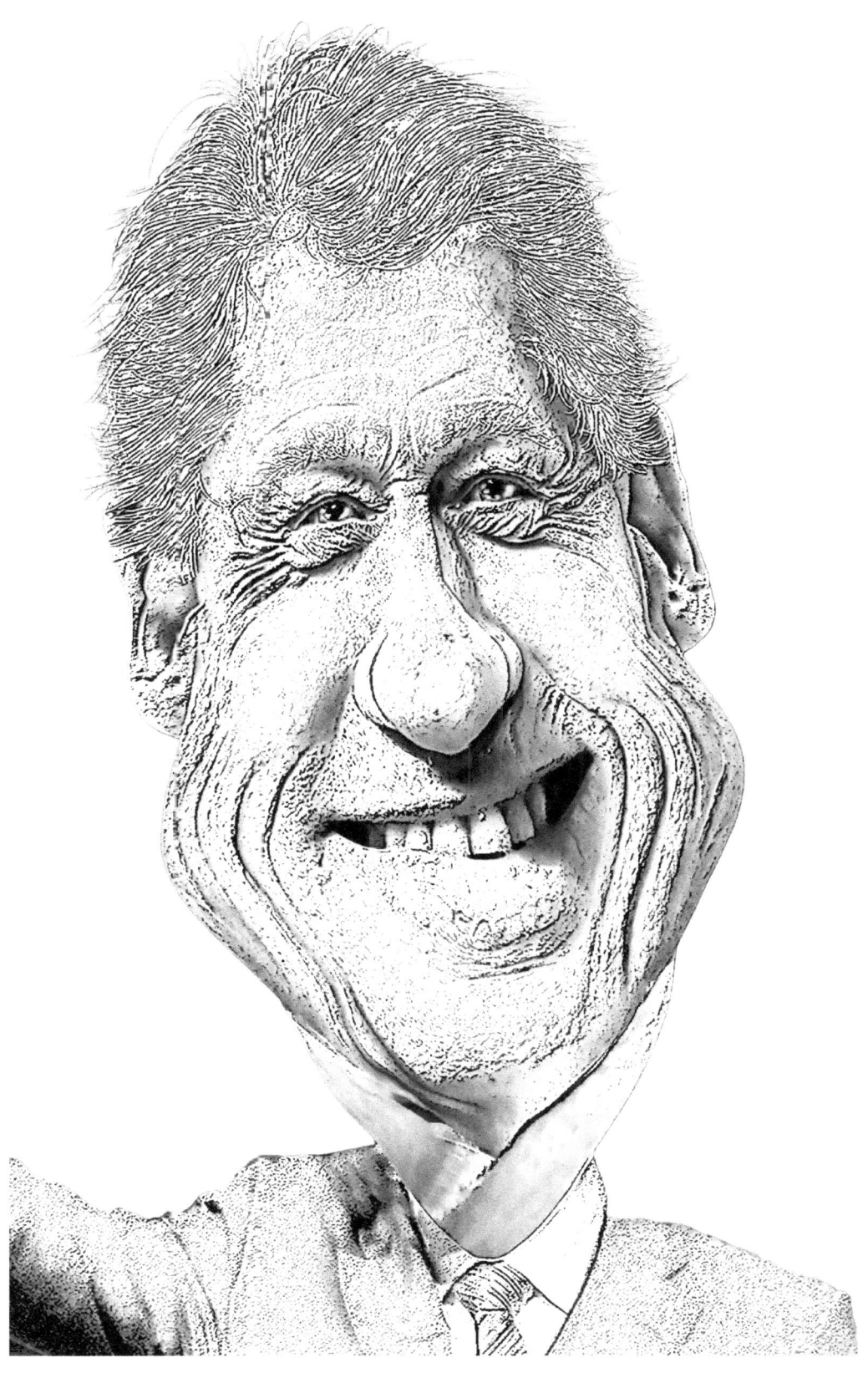

BILL CLINTON

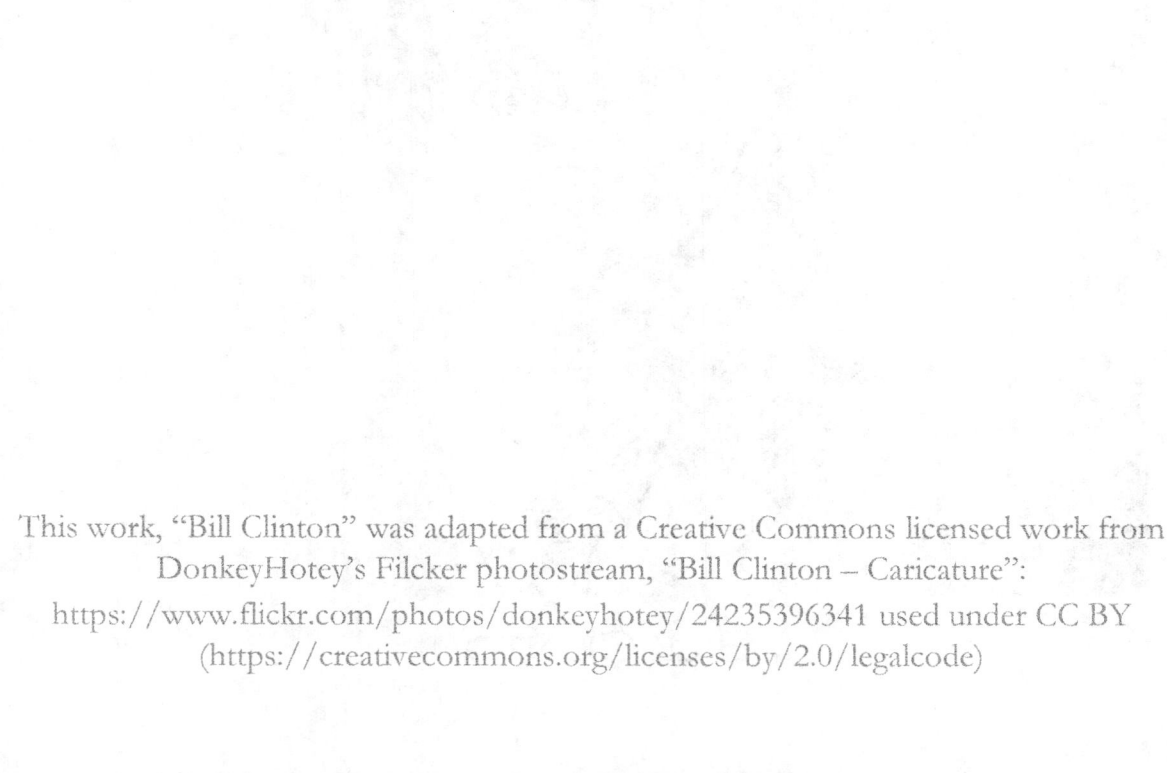

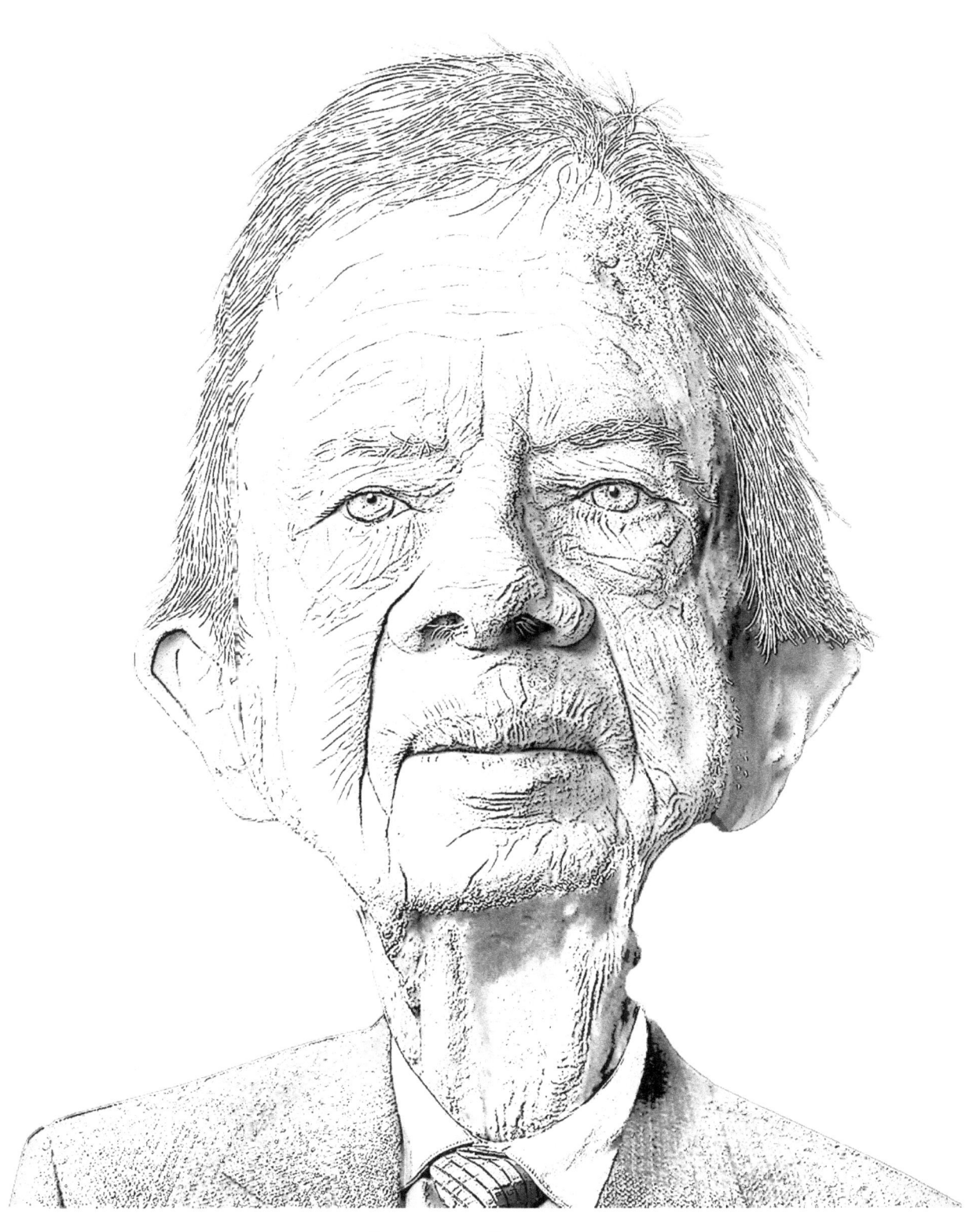

JIMMY CARTER

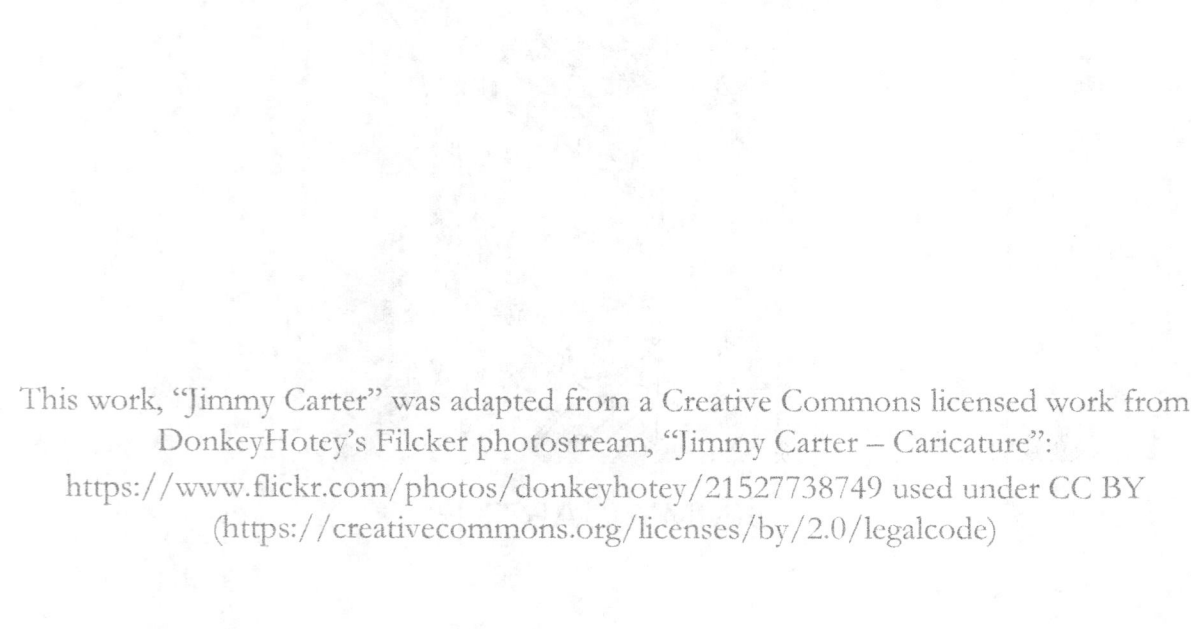

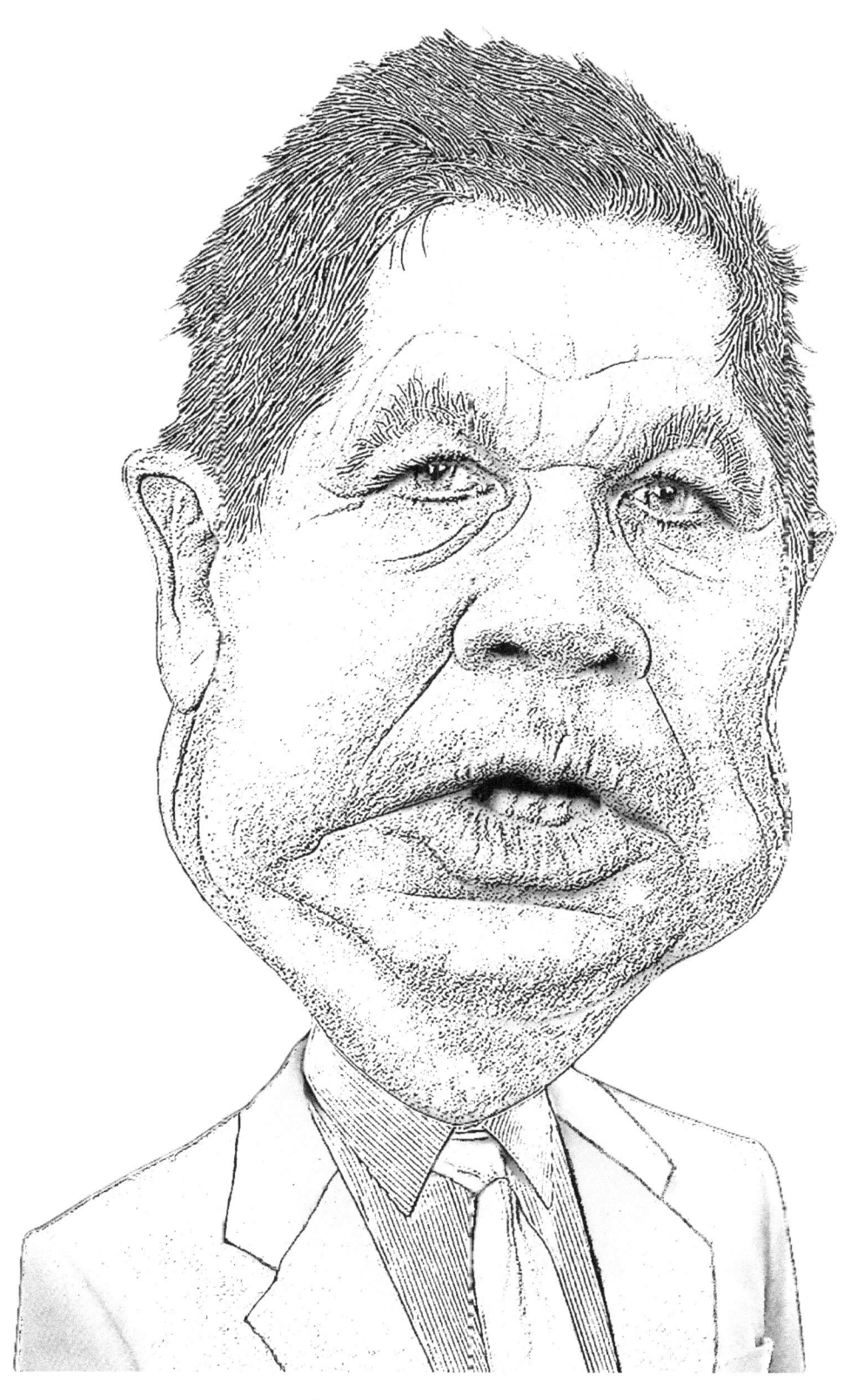

JOHN KASICH

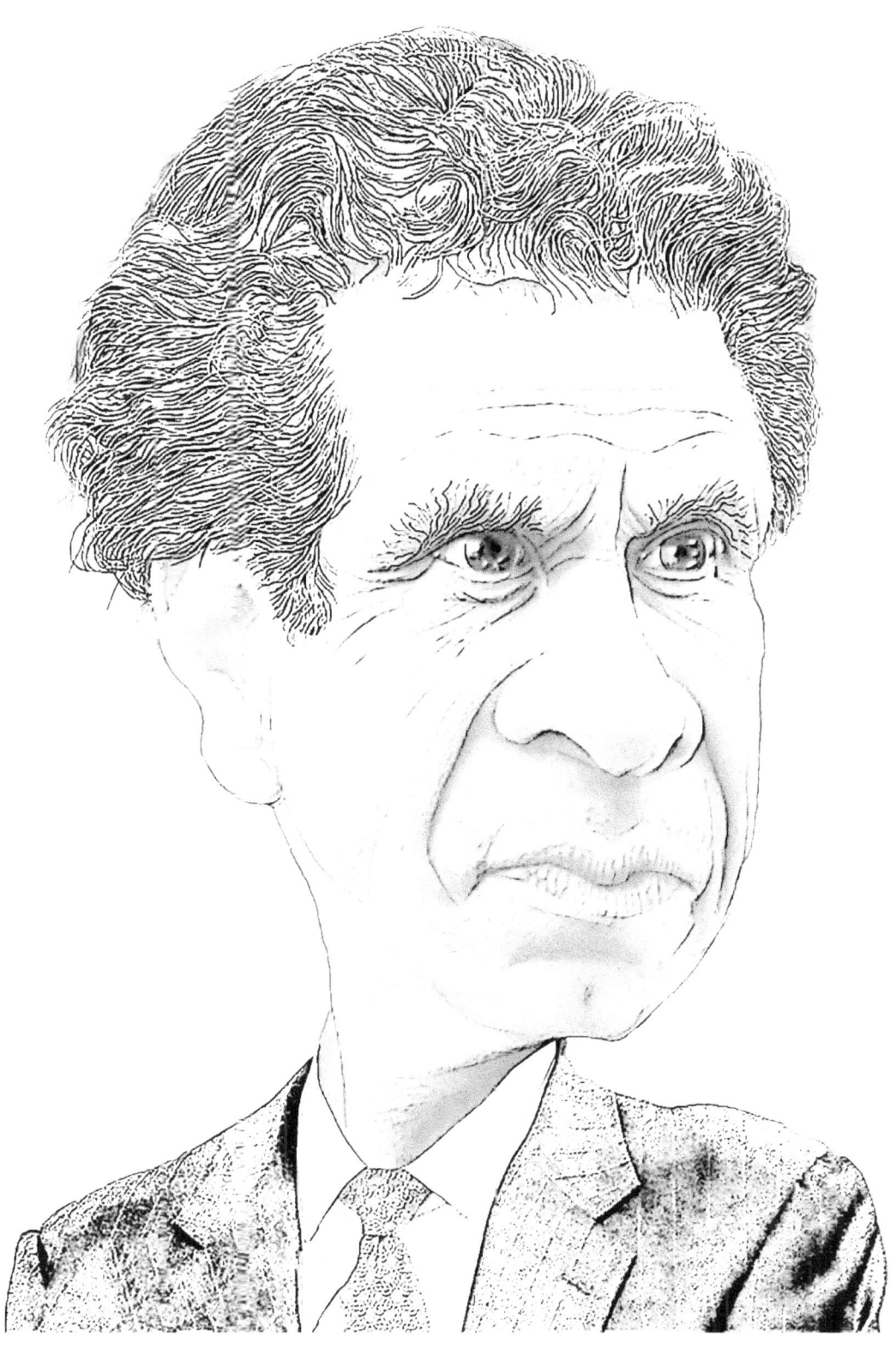

ANDREW CUOMO

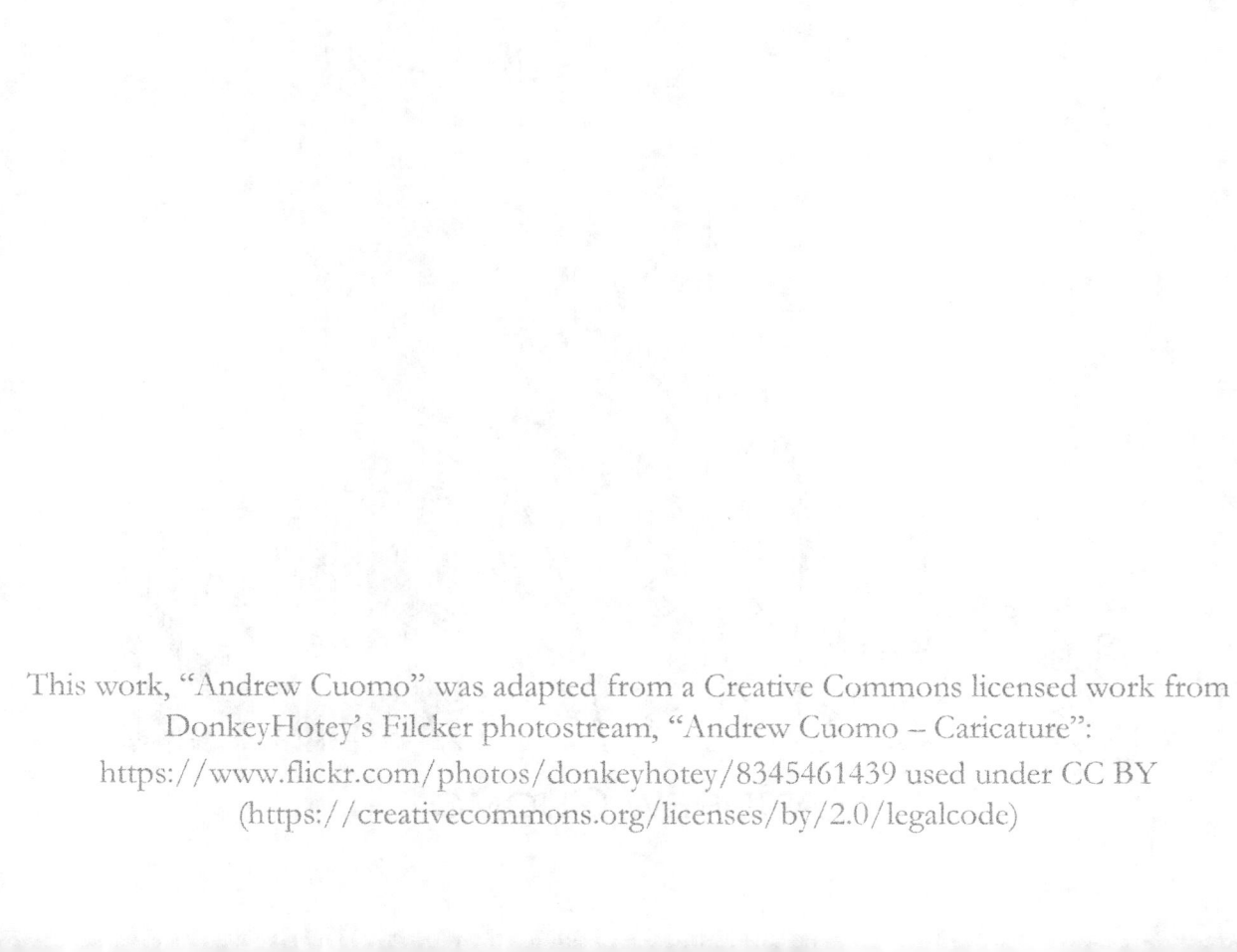

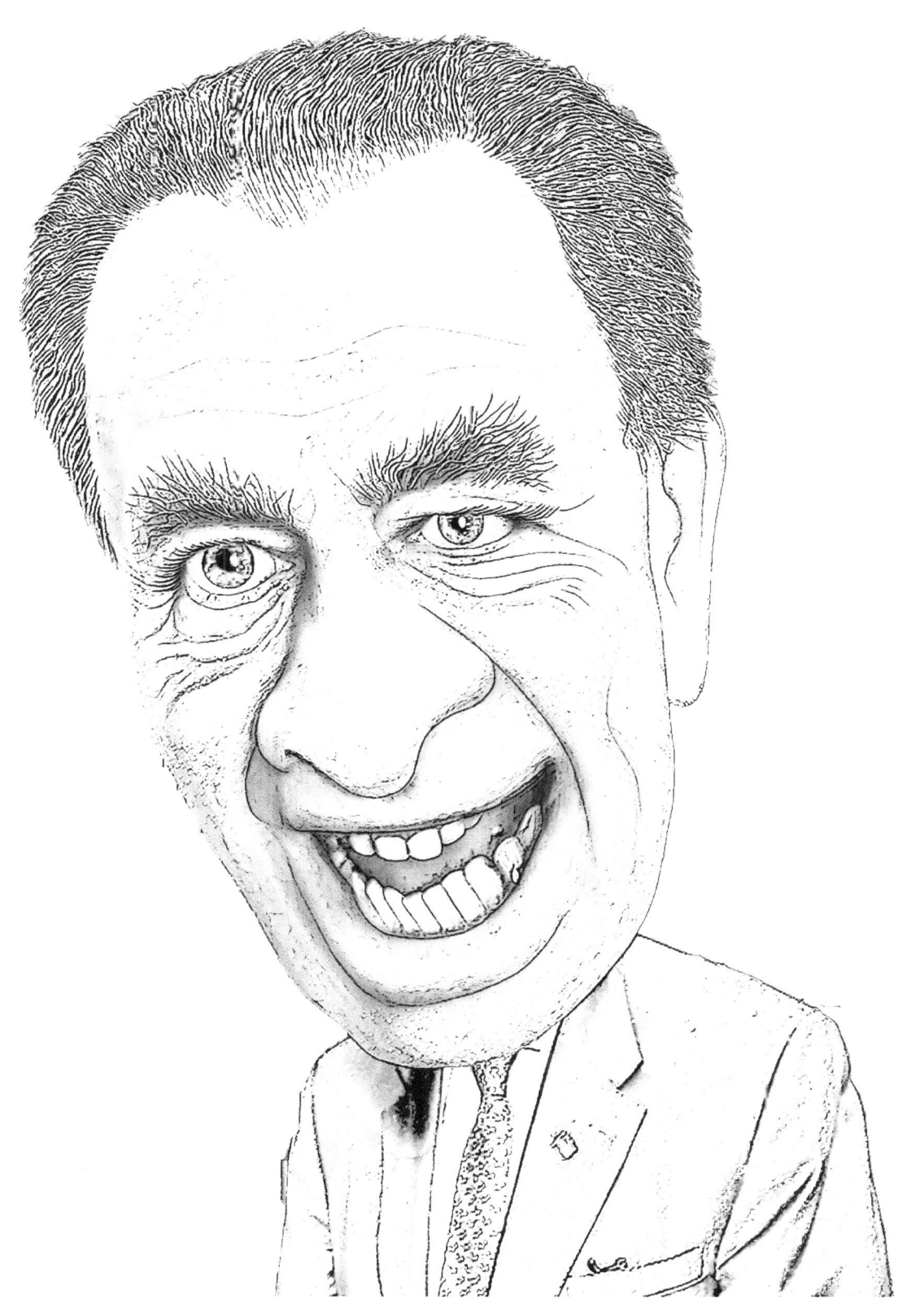

CHUCK SCHUMER

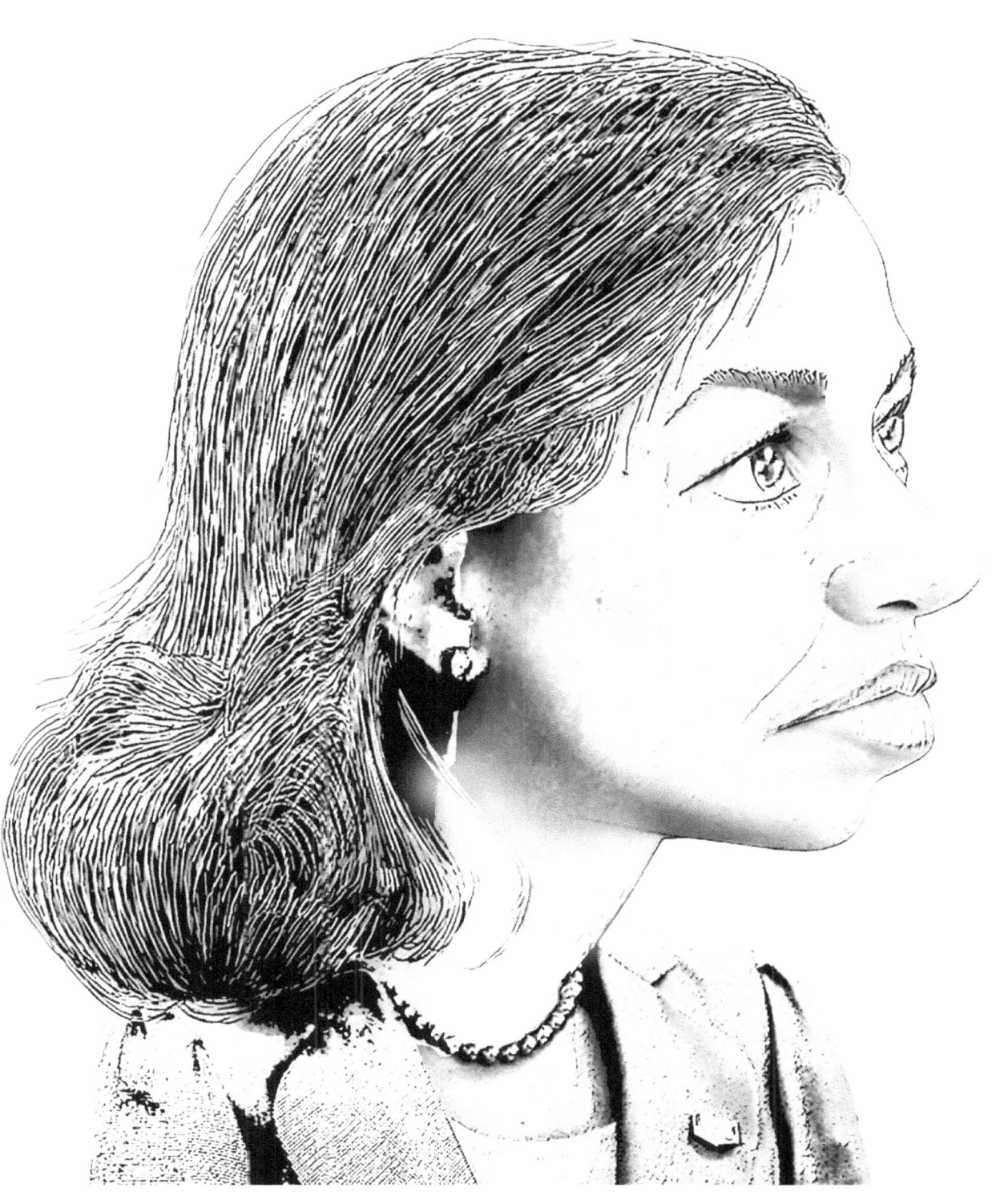

SUSAN RICE

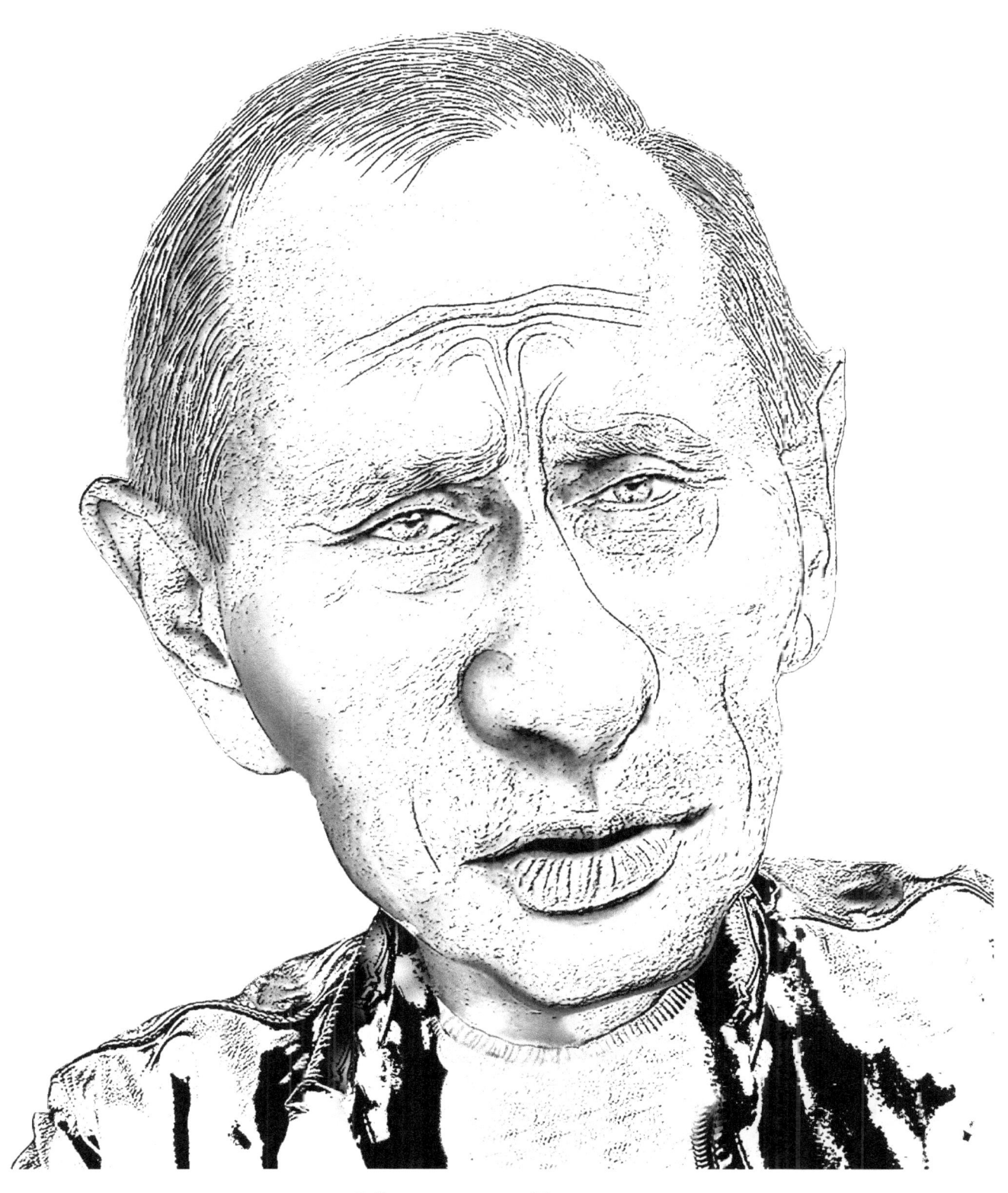

VLADIMIR PUTIN

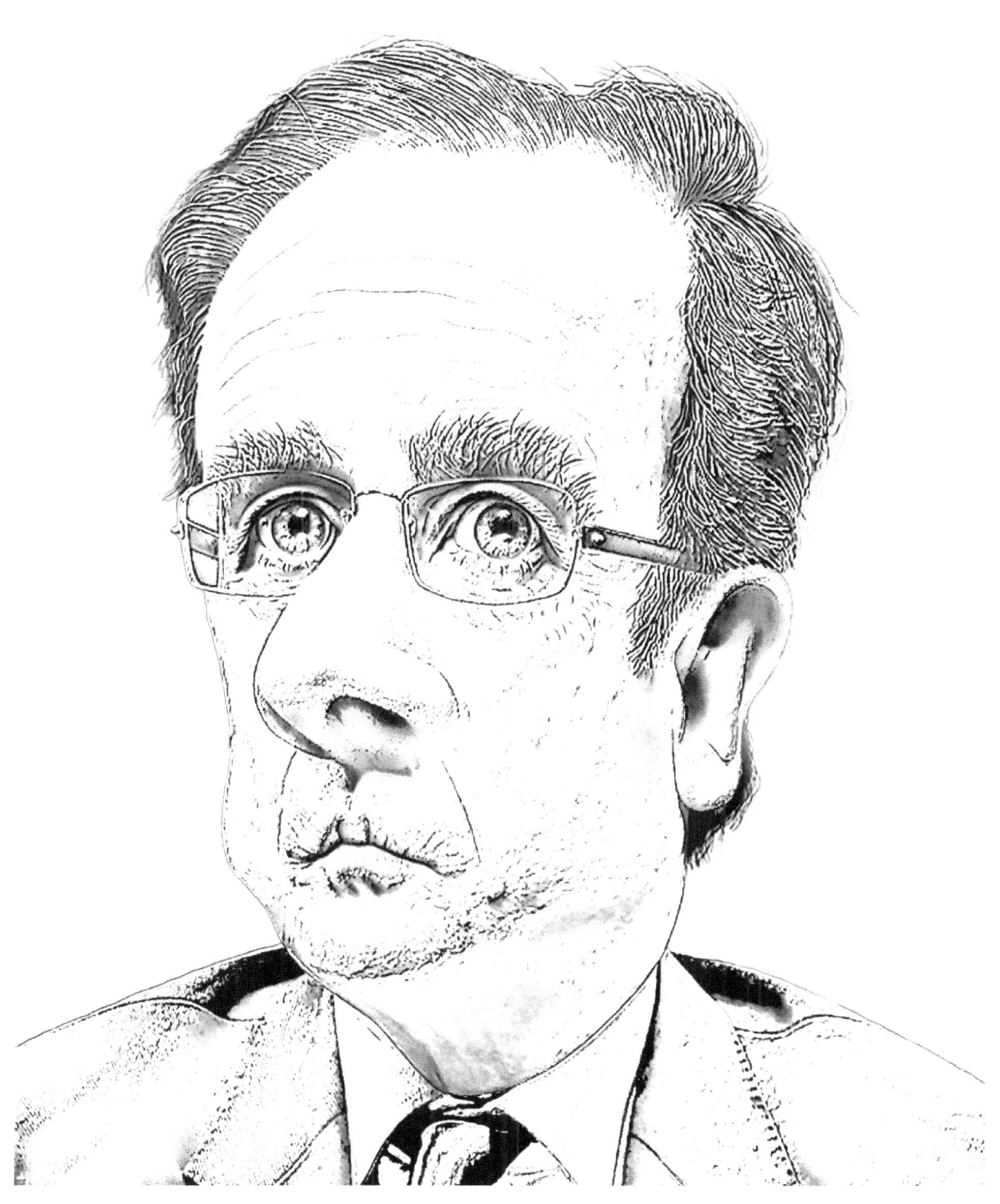

FRANCOIS HOLLANDE

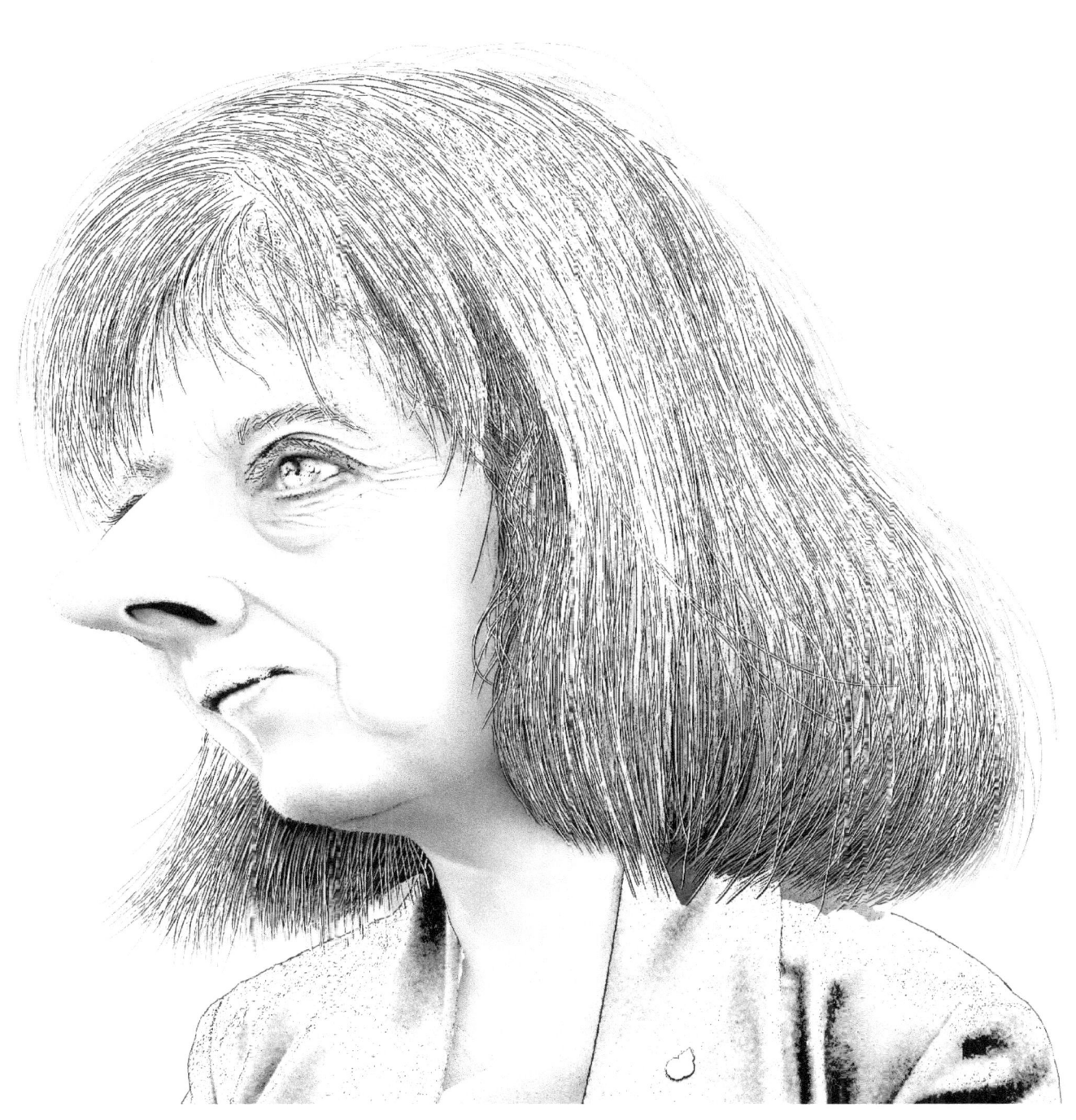

THERESA MAY

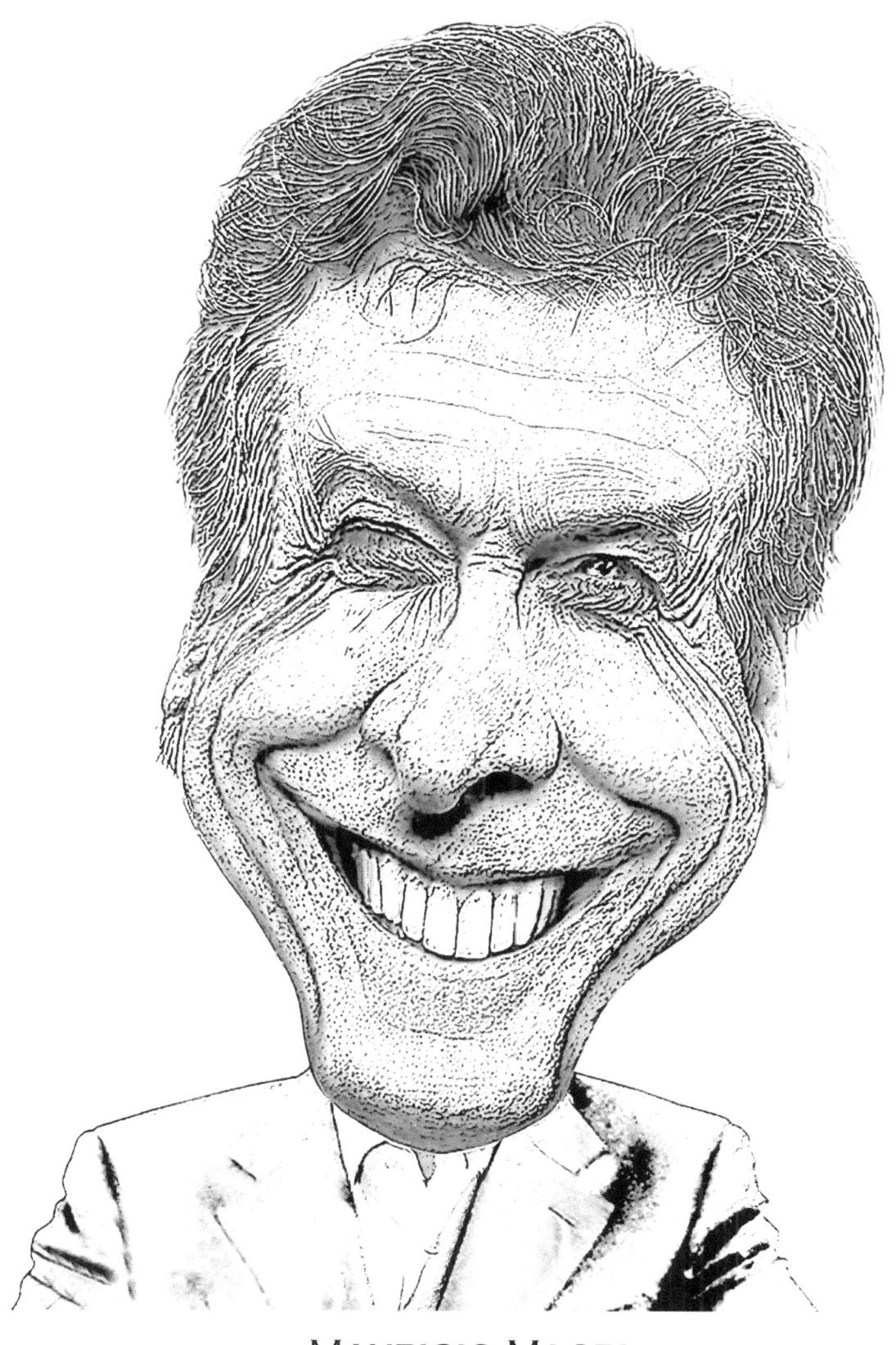

MAURICIO MACRI

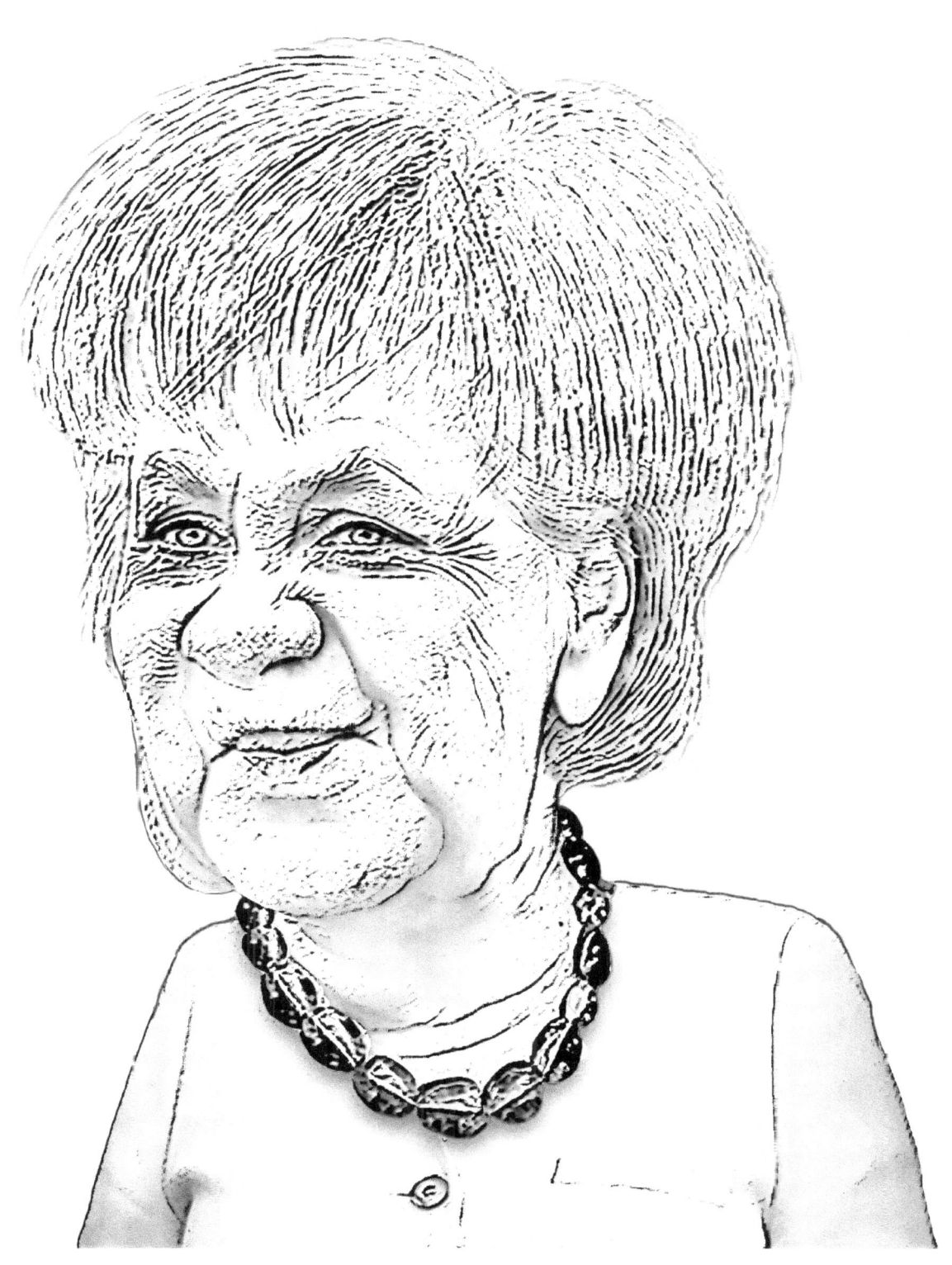

ANGELA MERKEL

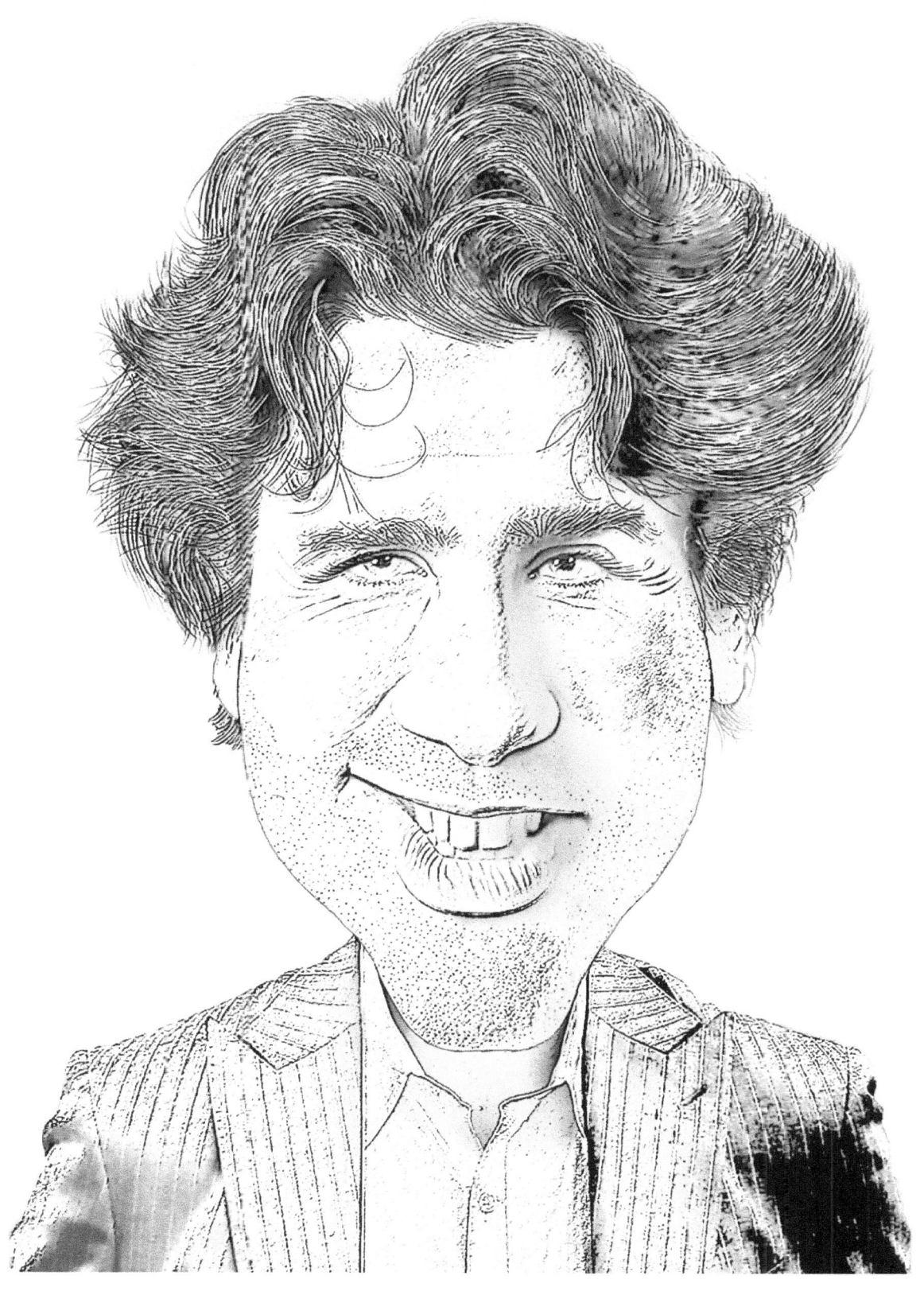

JUSTIN TRUDEAU

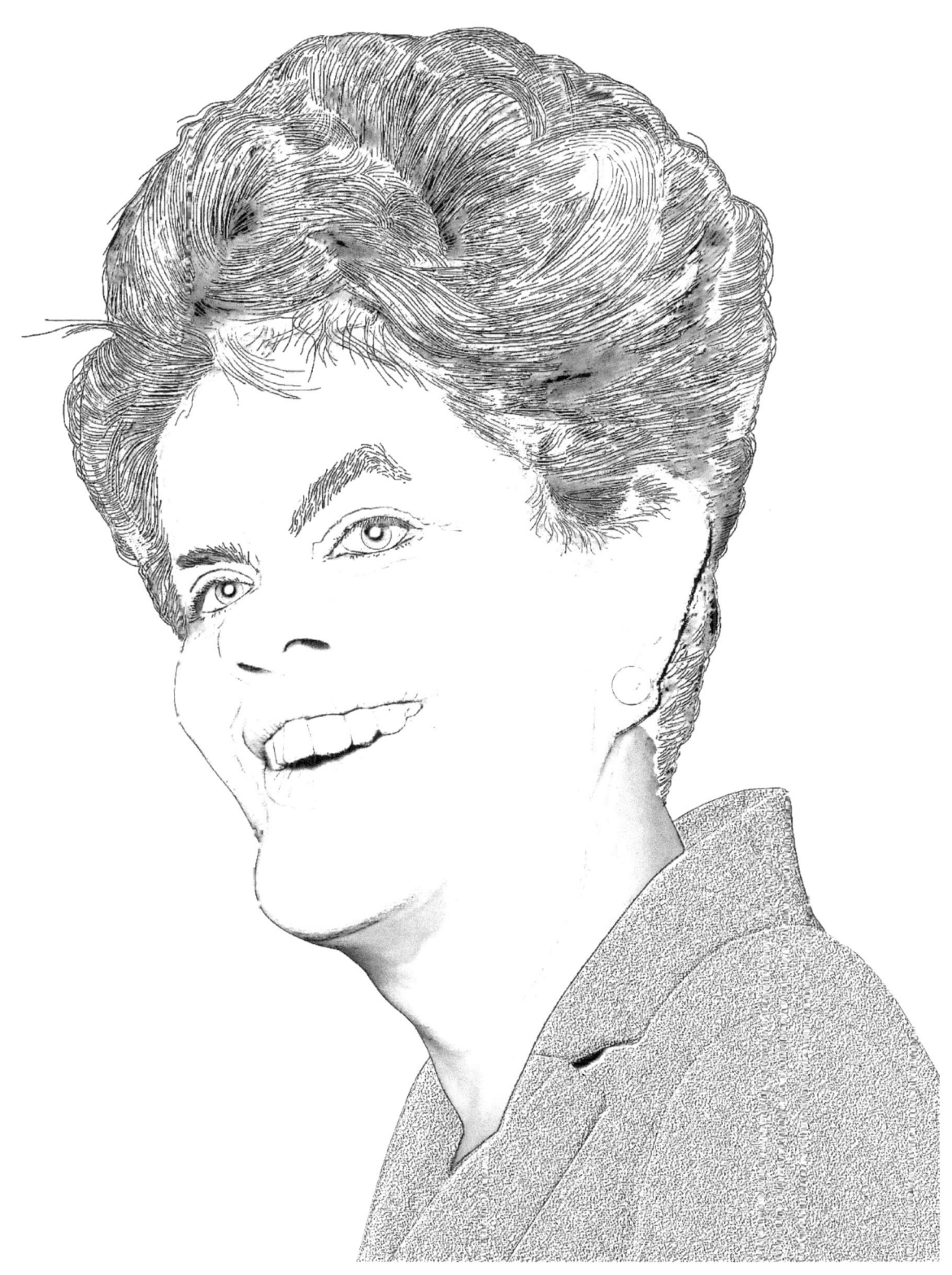

DILMA ROUSSEFF

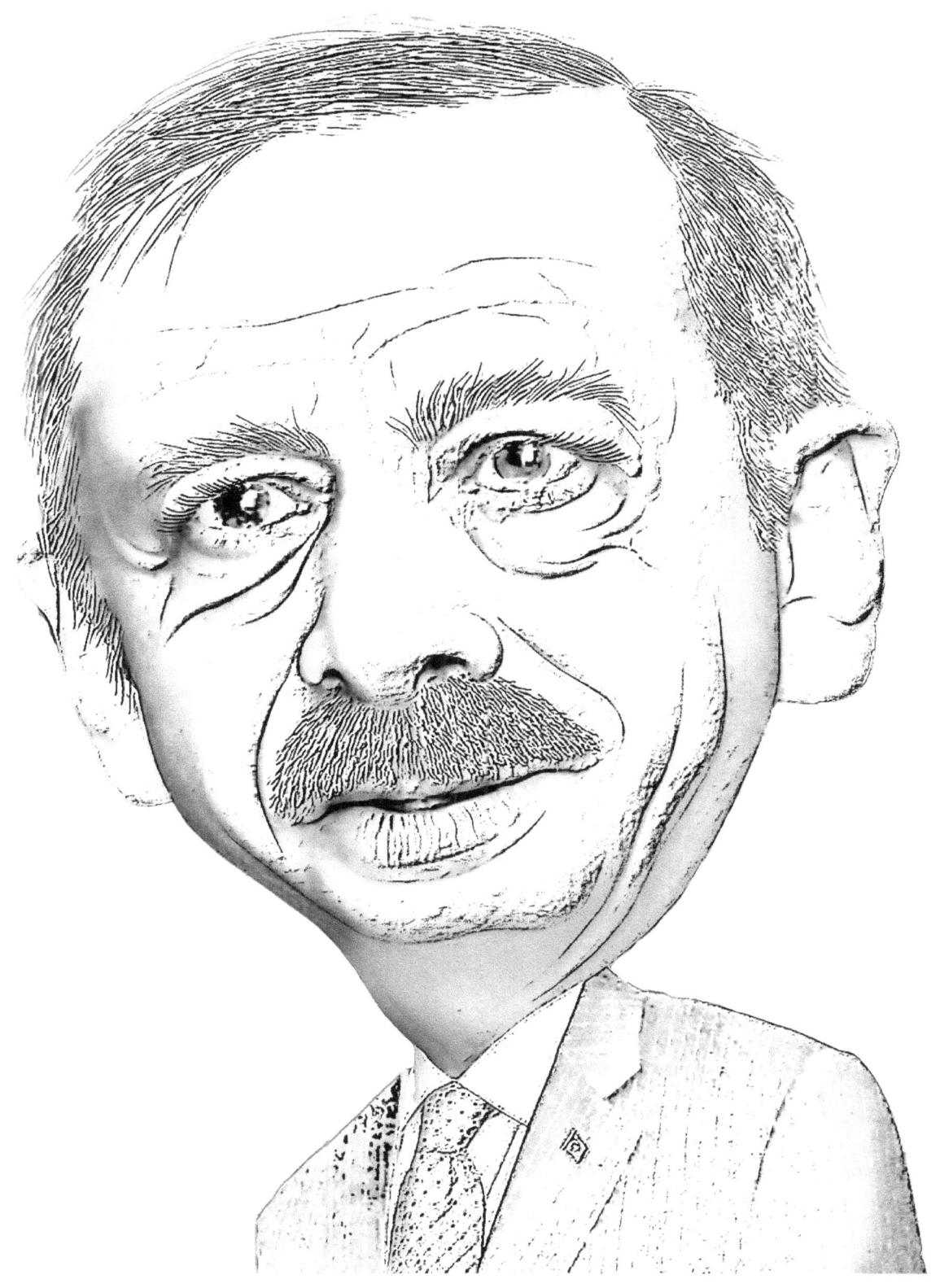

RECEP TAYYIP ERDOGAN

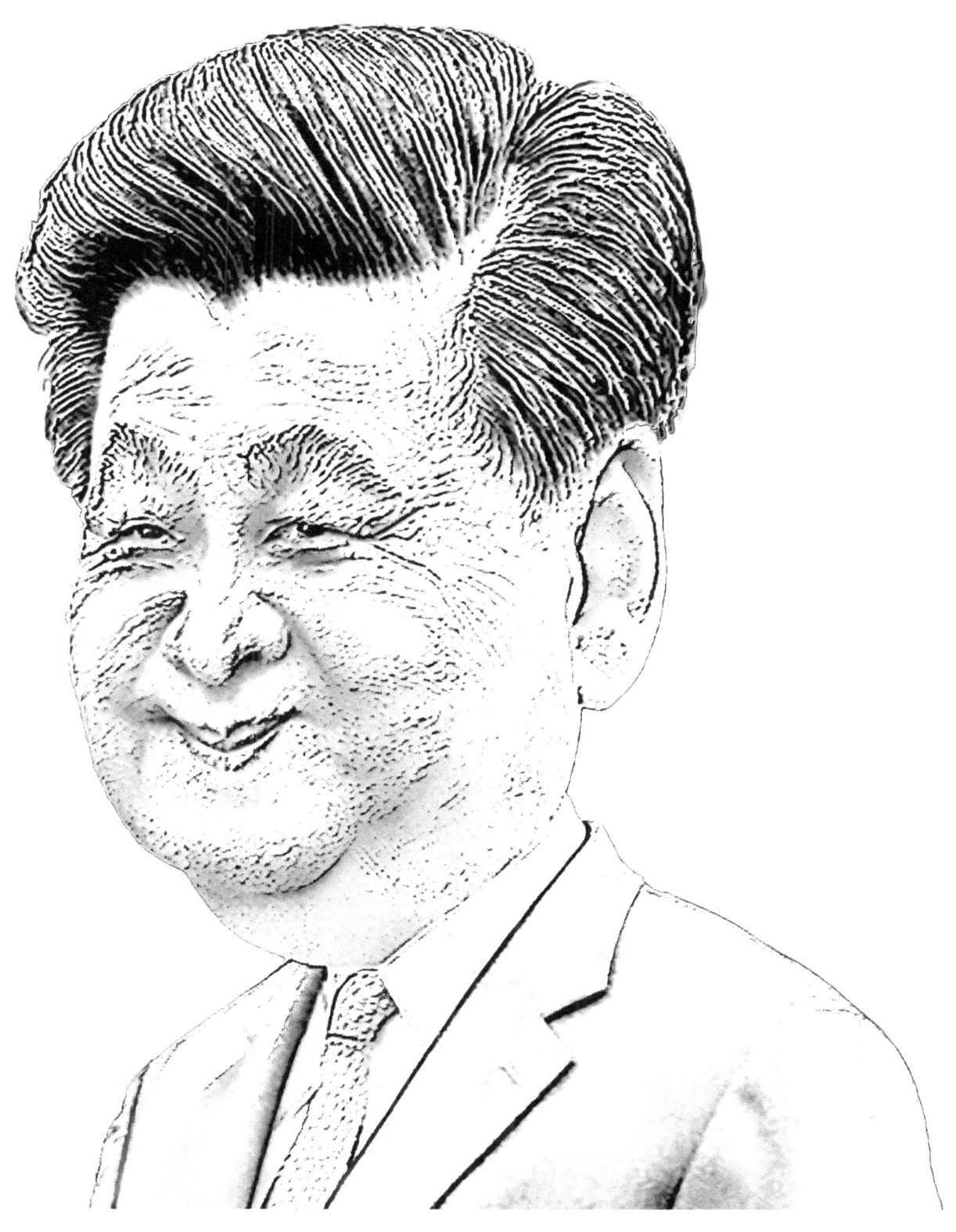

Xi Jinping

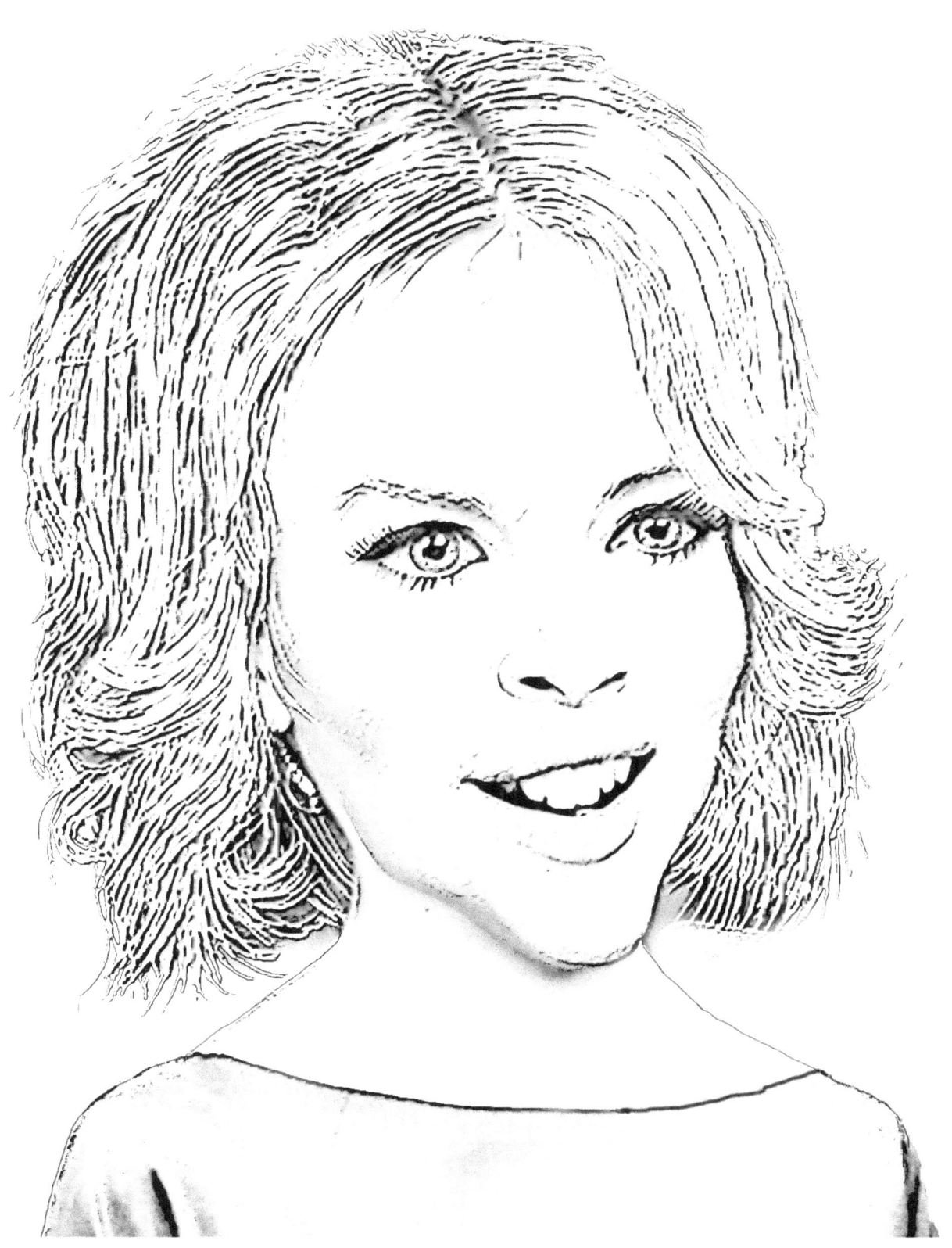

MEGYN KELLY

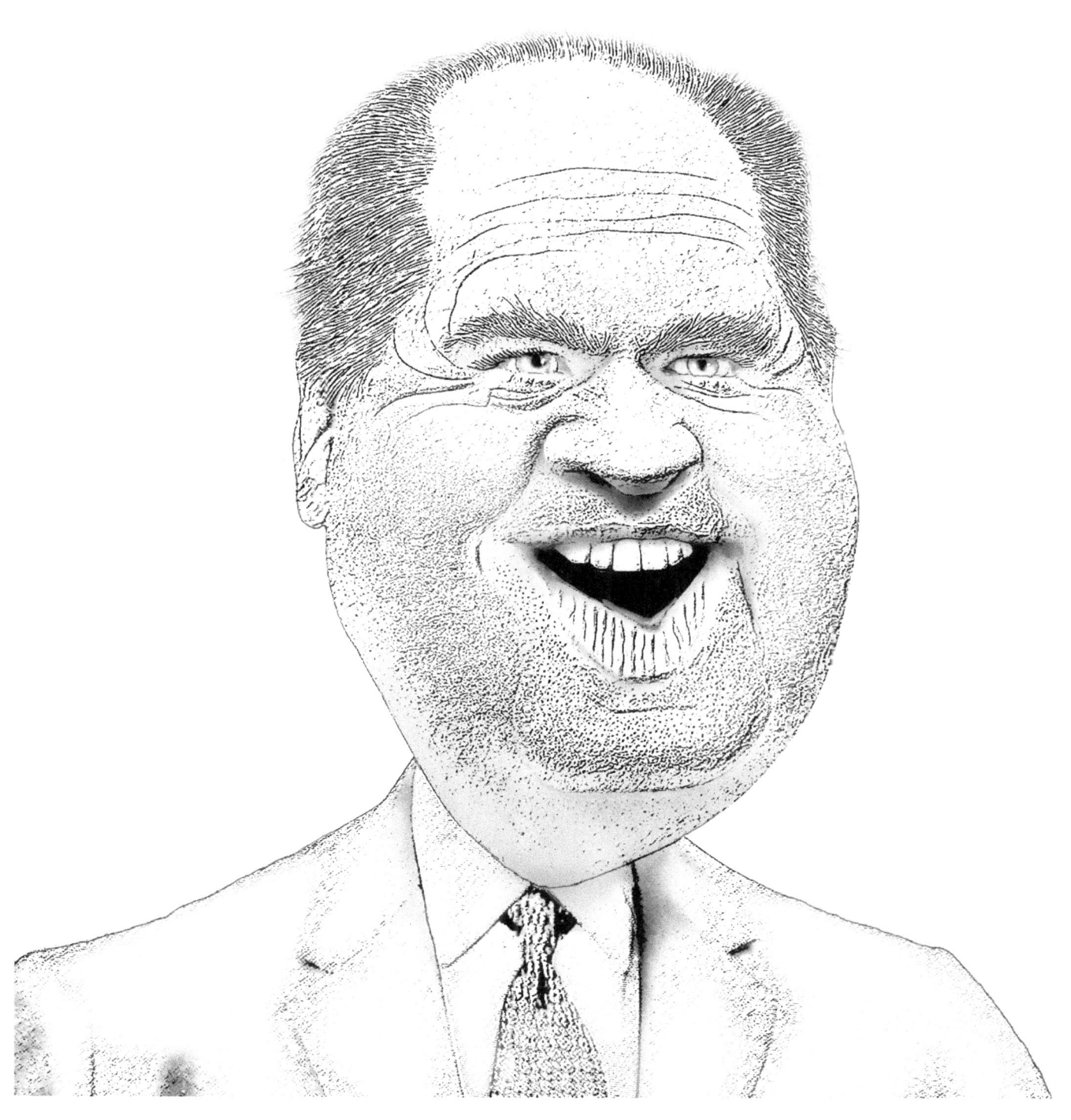

RUSH LIMBAUGH

www.ingramcontent.com/pod-product-compliance
Lightning Source LLC
Chambersburg PA
CBHW080539190526
45169CB00007B/2558

* 9 7 8 1 5 3 0 5 8 4 0 2 4 *